Charlie's
WOODS

George Reiker

To Dale,

I hope Charlies Woods will
open your heart to Gods love.
This book was inspired by my
own turmoil including divorce.
allow Gods love to guide and
Strengthen and give you hope

God Bless
George Reiker

Charlie's
WOODS

George Reiker

**Executive
Books**

Charlie's Woods

Published by
Executive Books
206 West Allen Street
Mechanicsburg, PA 17055
717-766-9499   800-233-2665
Fax: 717-766-6565
www.ExecutiveBooks.com

Cover Design and Interior Layout by Gregory A. Dixon

ISBN: 0-937539-95-3

Printed in the United States of America

DEDICATION

There are moments during our journey in life that God chooses to bless us by bringing someone very special into our lives when we need them most. Many people call them Guardian Angels, but no matter the title we give them, their arrival into our life changes it.

God so blessed my life with Charlie "Tremendous" Jones and it is to him I dedicate this book.

Charlie's genuine kindness and generosity, his love and friendship, and his living example of a life entrusted to Jesus Christ have been a major influence in my life and a source of inspiration for this book.

His love and appreciation for the precious gift of life, and his love for his fellowman are embodied by his love and devotion to our Lord and Savior. Charlie's testimony to Jesus Christ has touched the lives of thousands and thousands all over the world. He has remained a humble servant of God. He is a beacon of light in a dark world and a living testament to God's greatest commandment: Love one another as I have loved you. Here in lies the hope and future of mankind.

ACKNOWLEDGEMENT

This book would not be complete without expressing my deep gratitude and appreciation to all of those special people who contributed so much to this project.

I am so grateful to Bonnie and Charmaine who diligently typed the numerous rewrites with enthusiastic dedication.

A special thank you to Debbie, a very talented artist, who gave her valuable input from a creative standpoint.

To my dear friend John, who with persistent encouragement would not leave me rest until this book was complete. I give a very special thank you.

To my family and closest friends whose belief in me kept me writing.

My deepest and heartfelt gratitude to the love of my life, Veronica, who has worked tirelessly to keep our finances together, especially in the beginning. She has been a constant source of encouragement with her endless patience and unfaltering belief in me. She was the rock on this project, but also in my life.

TABLE OF CONTENTS

FOREWORD
By Charlie "Tremendous" Jones

FINDING YOUR PURPOSE is why you were born. Until that time you are not living, you are treading water, shadow boxing, existing. Finding your purpose is the beginning of life with a capital "L."

Passion follows purpose and purpose and passion will give meaning and profit to every success and failure the rest of your life.

As you read Ryan and Charlie's story, you'll discover the importance of a mentor. You'll discover the secret of great mentors is great ideals and ideas that were discovered in great biographies and devotionals. You'll see some of you in Ryan and hopefully some of you in his mentor. This is a simple story of how a bad experience turns into a life changing experience which might become your story. As the old saying goes, "when the student is ready, the teacher will arrive." I hope you will find your purpose as you share Ryan finding his.

"He is no fool who gives up what he can't keep to gain what he can never lose." **Jim Elliot**

CHAPTER 1

An air of uneasiness hung over my departure. Never before in my life had I planned a trip of this magnitude, especially on short notice. And the larger question still loomed over me. Why did I feel so compelled to go? Was there some divine power at work guiding me to the answers I so longed to find? Or was I just running away? A few short weeks ago my life was filled with love and hope, or so I thought. Then a series of events unfolded that turned my feelings of love and hope into fear and despair. My irrational fear of marrying Sarah had thrown me, releasing my feelings of insecurity and inadequacy that I had buried. Then the news from my doctor finally pushed me to the very edge. The terrible eye disease that had left so many of my relative's blind, had now infected me.

How was I to find the answers by taking this trip? Was this really the spiritual journey that Sarah tried to convince me it was? It was because of Sarah's compassionate urging that I finally decided to take this journey. My love for Sarah was so strong that I would try anything to rid myself of the anxiety and fear that paralyzed me, and maybe, Lord, I thought I'll discover somewhere in the wilderness why you have forsaken me. My mind was overloaded with these thoughts.

As we headed out the drive, Red, my Irish setter, was overjoyed, his tail wagging, head out the window. I didn't share in his excitement. In fact, I was questioning my very sanity for doing this. As we tuned onto the turnpike to head west, it started to rain. The sound of the wipers slowly faded as I got lost in my thoughts, the miles slipping away as if I were in a fog. My thoughts turned to Sarah. I could still see the tears in her eyes as we said our goodbyes. The memory of how she felt in my arms made my heart ache. Sarah had entered my life unexpectedly a year ago. Beautiful and bright, kind and gentle, loving and caring, Sarah was all these and more.

Introduced to each other by a mutual friend, this angelic lady helped to lift me out of my abyss of despair and stir the embers of love buried deep within my heart. I swore that I would never allow myself to fall in love again. I fought for months not to allow myself to get involved with her, but eventually she found her way into my heart. And it really scared me.

The sound of thunder jolted me out of my thoughts. I shook my head to clear the grogginess I felt. Red had just lain down with his head on my lap. I knew he could sense the depression I was in. I patted his head lightly. I was glad he was with me.

The sky started to clear as we neared the end of the Pennsylvania turnpike. About an hour into Ohio was the State Park we would be camping in for the night. We arrived at the campsite around 7:30. I set up the tent and started a fire. Red was busy sniffing every tree and rock in the area. At least he was enjoying himself.

I poured myself some coffee and sat by the fire, trying just to relax. Red lay down beside me. I could hear children playing and in the campsite next to me a couple sat snuggled together by a fire. I forced a smile. Dusk was setting in, and the crackling of the fire sent fiery ashes dancing into the air.

I leaned back in my chair and closed my eyes, lightly stroking Reds head as he sat next to me. I again wondered if I knew what I was doing taking this trip. Was this really some spiritual quest as Sara described it or was I just running from reality. For a long time I sat staring into the fire embraced by the darkness that surrounded me.

I laid out a blanket for Red to sleep on while I unrolled my sleeping bag. I checked the fire once as it was slowly dying down. I crawled into my sleeping bag and patted Red. "Boy, we have a long ways to go" I told him. He wagged his tail in approval. I laid my head back on my pillow, still stroking his back. From the door of the tent I could see the low dancing flames of the fire. A sense of loneliness set upon me, the same scary sense of totally being alone that had haunted me for so many years. I laid there wondering about this trip and what the future held. I was not feeling optimistic.

The next morning was sunny and cool. I packed up our things. I noticed a little restaurant down the road a few miles when we arrived the night before. We would stop for a quick breakfast and be on our way.

Over the next two days my despair continued to grow. A sense of depression consumed me as we passed through one state after another, most of the time not remembering anything along the way. I was a prisoner of my own thoughts. The events of the past several weeks would replay themselves over and over again in my mind.

The total unraveling of my life, the strange dreams that now filled my sleep, and an unexplainable compelling desire to go to Montana now consumed my waking hours. Sarah believed my guardian angel was in Montana calling me. I didn't put any faith in that. All I knew at the age of forty was that my life was a terrible mess.

By Wednesday we were halfway to Montana. My thoughts turned to the letter I had sent Sarah. She should get it today. Will any of my words make sense to her? Will it help her to understand me as a man? I wondered how over the past year I could feel so alive and filled with love, and then a fateful series of events could so suddenly stir up my feelings of insecurity and worthlessness. I couldn't even turn to God for help, because I was sure he wasn't even listening to me. Was He even real? What was the purpose of my being here anyhow? I was sinking deeper and deeper into a pool of hopelessness. I struggled to fight it, but everything I had learned over the years from countless self-help books and motivational seminars was deserting me now. My lifeline to reality was quickly becoming frayed.

I was in no mood to camp out again. I just didn't have the

energy. Around 9:30 we came to a motel just off the highway and I pulled over and went inside. The office was quaint and clean. I paid for a room. The manager was very friendly and I'm sure I didn't hide very well the depressing mood I was in. "Hey!" he said as I opened the door to leave " I don't mind your dog sleeping in your room," he smiled. I thanked him and walked out.

I grabbed my bag and called Red to follow me. I put the key in the lock and opened the door, I tossed my bag on the chair and put some water in a bowl for Red, and then I just fell on the bed, exhausted, quickly falling asleep.

I awoke Thursday morning feeling tired. My sleep had been filled with a crazy array of dreams. Again I dreamed of the old man, telling me he would be sent to save me. Even sleep now was no refuge. I drove all day Thursday. I wanted to reach my destination in Montana by Friday evening. Steve, a dear friend had arranged for me to stay at his grandfather's cabin. There I could find solitude, but that thought didn't really excite me.

Friday morning we crossed over the border to Montana. I felt a sense of uneasiness, and the feeling of despair wouldn't go away. The pool of self pity I had slipped into was slowly swallowing me up. By noon I was struggling to stay awake, so I pulled off the highway to rest for a while. I laid back the drivers seat and closed my eyes. Red put his nose against my cheek. Good boy I said patting his head. "We're going to rest awhile before we head on. Now lay down" I said softly. He nuzzled me again and then lay down in the back seat.

Again I had the strangest dream. I had been hiking and had come to a cliff. Red was dancing around me and lost his footing on the edge and fell off. I dove to grab him, but I missed. I started to scream, when all of the sudden Red came floating back to the top of the cliff, as if held by some invisible force. As I looked in disbelief, a voice came from behind me. "Stay true to the path I've put you on and have faith in me." There was a blinding light and then it was gone. Then I felt a hand on my shoulder. I turned and jumped back in surprise. Standing before me was the old man. "Who are you?" I asked still shaken by his appearance.

"Who I am is not important now. Know that when you have reached the edge of your cliff in life and are about to slip over, I will be sent to save you."

"Save me from what?" I asked. Again he did not answer, and he turned and walked away.

I started to chase after him screaming, "Save me from what?"

He turned and answered in a deep voice "From your disbelief."

Then he just disappeared. I stood there trying to understand his answer. Red was barking where the old man had vanished. The barking grew louder and louder. Someone was tapping my shoulder.

"Sir, sir wake up. Are you okay?" I woke from the deep state of sleep I had fallen in. I slowly focused my eyes to see a man in uniform standing outside my car. I jerked up in my seat startled. "It's okay sir. I'm with the Montana Highway Patrol. Is everything okay here?"

Shaking my head I answered, "Yes, officer, everything is alright. I must have fallen asleep. I pulled off to rest and must have dozed off."

"You were really out of it, it took me awhile to wake you. You haven't been drinking, have you?" I looked at him bewildered at first.

"No, no. Just having a bad dream."

He opened my door "Why don't you walk around and get some blood circulating," he said. "I saw you were from out of state so I stopped to see if you needed some assistance," he added.

"I'm tired," I mumbled. I told him where I was going, and he confirmed that I still had about a 3 hour drive ahead of me. He reminded me to stay alert and gave Red a pat on the head, wished me luck, and drove off.

I let Red out of the car. He ran a short distance smelling

everything. I leaned back against the car, the warmth of the sun shining down on my face.

My despair had become so overwhelming that I hadn't even noticed the beauty that now surrounded me. I was still shaken from my dream. What did it all mean, or was it just a stupid dream? I certainly felt I was hanging from an emotional cliff. And how could this old man, this stranger save me? I wondered if I was losing my mind. Had I already fallen over the edge? I called Red back to the car and pulled onto the highway. The more I drove the more uncertain I became. Whatever it was I had come out here searching for, I certainly hadn't found it yet. In fact I felt more alone, more depressed than when I had left. If this was some spiritual journey I wanted no more of it. "What am I dong here?" I thought.

About 4:30 I came upon a tavern housed in a large log cabin. I don't know why, but I decided to stop. I definitely could use a drink. I parked at the edge of the parking lot down by the trees so Red would be in the shade. The evening was turning cool, so I knew he'd be okay in the car, and I wasn't going to be long anyhow. The place started to become more crowded as the evening went on. Before I knew it several hours had passed and though the alcohol helped numb the pain, it did absolutely nothing for my depression. I decided to leave and headed for the door.

As I neared the car Red started barking frantically. I thought he was just excited to see me. I told him to calm down, when I heard footsteps behind me. Before I could turnaround, I felt a sharp pain to the side of my head. I fell to the ground and things got fuzzy. I could still hear Red's barking and muffled voices. I tried to get up, but couldn't. Then I felt someone kick me in the chest. I pulled myself up on my hands and knees, gasping for breath, when they kicked me several more times, then another blow to my head. I was losing consciousness as I felt someone going through my pockets. Then everything went black.

CHAPTER 2

When I awoke my head was exploding in pain. I felt a strange numbness in my arms and legs. It hurt to even breathe. My vision was blurred as I tried to focus on where I was. I groaned in pain. "Be still." I heard a deep, but gentle voice say. A figure stood beside me. I strained to see and slowly my eyes adjusted to the world around me. An old gentleman was next to my bed.

"Who are you?" I whispered. "Where am I?"

"Try to be still," he replied. "My name is Pete. I'm a doctor."

"What happened?" I moaned.

"You've been beaten pretty badly." He answered. "But you'll be all right"

I tried to sit up and excruciating pain shot through me. "Don't try to sit up," the old doc instructed." Your ribs are badly bruised and you have a deep laceration on your head. You need rest." He turned to the door. "Charlie, Charlie!" he yelled. "Come in here."

I laid there feeling like a Mac truck had run over me. Never had I experienced pain like I was feeling now. I was still groggy. I heard footsteps walk to the doorway. My vision was fuzzy as I strained to see who the doctor was talking to.

He was a tall, big man. "Has our friend come around?" I heard him say to the doctor. The voice seemed strangely familiar. He walked over to where I was laying. "How are you doing friend?" he asked in a burley voice. I stared at him in disbelief.

17

I couldn't get any words to come out of my mouth. I rubbed my eyes and opened them again. The clothes were different, but this was the old man in my dreams. No, it couldn't be. My mind raced for an explanation, an answer. The old man noticed the look on my face. "Don't be afraid, you're among friends. Doc here says you're going to be okay." he said. Surprisingly, his words, his voice reassured me.

"My dog, is my dog okay?" I gasped.

"Yes, he's fine," the old man answered. "He's lying right here on the floor next to your bed."

"Red, thank God you're okay." His tail wagged against the floor at the sound of his name.

"I've given you something for the pain," the Doc said. "Now it took 23 stitches to close the cut on your head, so you're going to have a good headache for a day or two….and there's a chance you've suffered a concussion. Charlie is going to keep a close eye on you through the night."

"Who did this?" I groaned.

"Don't know," Charlie answered. "They took off when your dog clawed his way out of the car. That's all I saw." He added. "You're not going to be able to travel for awhile, at least several weeks," the Doc said. The pain medication was kicking in and I was fading fast.

"Charlie will take good care of you," I heard the doc say. "You're a lucky man he came by when he did. Now get plenty of rest." These were the last words I heard.

When I awoke the old man was sitting beside my bed. He closed the book he was reading and walked over to me. My head felt like a train was running through it. "Oh, my head" I moaned.

"Welcome back to the real world," the old man said with a smile. "You had us a little worried." he added.

"Why? How long have I been asleep?" I asked.

"Nearly two days," he answered. "The doc was here yesterday, but he didn't wish to disturb you, so he told me to keep a close eye on you."

"You've been sitting here the whole time?" I asked.

"Pretty much," he answered.

He got up to pour some water. "Try to drink some," he said.

As I tried to sit up the pain in my chest knocked me back down.

"Here try this," he said, concerned, putting another pillow under my head. "You're still in a lot of pain, aren't you? These pills the doc left should give you some relief. Also, I've prepared some soup for you. Now take these pills while I go get it," he said firmly.

As I watched him leave the room, I still couldn't get over how much he was like the old man in my dream. Nonsense, I thought. I looked around the room I was in. It was simply furnished. I assumed he lived in a log house by the wood floor and ceiling and log walls. The room was neat and clean. Red lay on the rug by the bed.

I looked through the bedroom doorway out into the living area. I could only see the far wall, and it was filled with books. I wondered, who was this kind old man who without hesitation, was willing to care for a stranger?

Then it struck me. I promised Sarah I would call her and let her know I had arrived okay. If I had slept for the past two days, today had to be Monday and I told Sarah I would call her on Friday or Saturday at the latest. She had to be wondering why I hadn't called.

The old man came in with a tray. I could smell the aroma from the soup.

"Sir, I need to call my girlfriend. She has to be worried." I said frantically. He looked at me and smiled.

"We've already contacted her," he replied. "She knows you're okay."

"How? Who called her?" I asked.

His big hand rubbed his chin. "You don't remember do you?' he asked.

"Remember what?" I replied.

"Well, you were really out of it, you kept mumbling something about calling a Sarah. I kept you conscious long enough to get her telephone number from you."

"No I don't remember," I commented. "Is she okay?" I asked.

"She's fine, but very concerned about you. I assured her that you would be alright.

He leaned over and kissed my cheek. I looked at him strangely. "She asked me to give you that." The old man said with a smile. "She sounds like a special lady," he added.

"She is, she really is." I answered. "She also said that she would contact your friend so he could tell his grandfather that you wouldn't be arriving for several weeks."

Great I thought, as I sipped some soup. I came all the way out here in search of who knows what, and I wind up getting beaten up by a couple of punks. What was the purpose of all this, I thought.

The more I saw and heard this old man, the more I sensed a connection to him. And oddly, I felt I belonged here. None of this made any sense.

I heard a knock at the door. "Hi, c'mon in," I heard the old man say. "Your patient is waiting for you."

The doctor walked into my room. "How are you doing today?" he asked cheerfully.

"I still feel pretty rough," I answered, "but my head doesn't hurt quite as much."

"Good, good," he said, as he checked me over. "We'll take those stitches out in a few days," he said. "I can see Charlie's been taking good care of you," he added.

"Yes, yes he has," I replied. "I'm very grateful to both of you. Can I ask you a question doc?" I motioned for him to close the door.

"Who is Charlie?" I asked. "And why is he being so kind to me?"

"Oh, Charlie is a dear and a special friend," he replied. I could see the love he felt for this man by his expression and his comments. "Don't worry, son," he said to me. "You're in very special company."

"How so?" I asked.

"Oh," he said smiling. "Old man Charlie is one of God's angles on earth."

I stared at him, my eyes questioning his comment. "You'll find out in time, trust me my friend." He told me he'd be back in a couple of days and to get plenty of rest. He opened the bedroom door to leave and then turned around. "You want to know where you are?" he said. He looked at me for a moment. Then he smiled. "Welcome to Charlie's Woods," he said as he turned and closed the door.

"Charlie's Wood's," I said out loud. "What's Charlie's Woods?"

CHAPTER 3

Over the next couple of days I slept a lot. The old man took care of me cheerfully, preparing my meals, and helping me in and out of bed and putting up with my moods.

There was definitely something different about this old man. He had a genuine gentleness and kindness that just flowed from him. Though I had stayed with him just these couple of days, I couldn't shake the feeling that I had known him a long time.

The doc was right, and though I didn't understand or have an explanation for my feelings, I felt I was in very special company. I was tired of lying in bed, so the old man helped me into the living room. Well, it was more like a living room/dining area. Though I was still in much pain, it felt good to be out of bed.

Charlie went into the kitchen to make some tea. I looked around the room. In the center of one wall was a stone fireplace with two rocking chairs, one on each side. All the walls were filled with books—I mean lots and lots of books. A picture of the crucifixion of Christ hung over the fireplace. As my eyes met the picture, an unexplainable feeling of sadness swept over me.

Charlie came back in the room interrupting my thoughts. He sat down a cup of tea, and sat in the chair across from me. "Beautiful painting isn't it?" he said, eyeing the picture I had been staring at.

"Yes, it is," I said, yes it is."

"How's your tea?" he asked.

"It's very good," I answered. "What kind is it?"

"Oh a special brew of my own," he replied, proudly. "It's good for the soul," he added.

Well I need plenty of this, I thought.

Red came over and sat next to me. I patted his head. "I think I owe you a big thank you," I said rubbing his head.

"He's a beautiful dog," Charlie commented, "and I can tell he loves you very much. He probably saved your life," he added.

"He's pretty special to me too," I replied.

"Well, he and I have become good friends," the old man said, "but he wouldn't come out of your room except to go out. You must be very special, Ryan, to have an animal bond with you like that."

I nodded and the words came out, though I don't know why. "I don't feel very special." As I sat looking down at the table I could feel the old man's eyes staring at me.

"I sense you are troubled," he said kindly. "Would you like to talk about it?" he asked. I shook my head no. Suddenly the reality of my life came flooding back and the heaviness of my despair landed on my shoulders. I felt terribly alone sitting here in a strange home in the middle of nowhere.

He reached his large hands across the table and placed them gently over mine. Compassion filled his voice as he spoke. "Son, I am here to help, trust in me." Those words "trust in me" shot through me like a bolt of lightening. I stared at the old man, and started trembling. He squeezed my hands. Could he know what I didn't know, understand what I didn't understand? Suddenly I was overwhelmed, the dreams, the voices, the feelings, they were all too much for me to comprehend. But a connection was made.

I sat there unable to speak. My cup danced to the edge of the table from my trembling and crashed to the floor. Inside I was screaming, but not a single word fell from my lips. Slowly I pulled myself up out of my chair.

I apologized to the old man for the broken cup. "Charlie, I need to go and lie down, I mumbled. "I don't feel very well." The old man gently helped me to my bed, and then closed the door behind him. I lay down in my bed alone trying to catch my breath. I wanted to run, but physically couldn't. I was stuck here. But where was here? Was I in a spiritual haven or the twilight zone? This was too bizarre to make any rational sense.

As I slowly calmed down, my thinking became more rational. "Trust in me," as I heard him say those words again in my mind, a real calmness came over me. It made no sense, but I felt I could trust the old man.

How could I feel trust with an old man I just met a week ago? I wondered if the answers I sought were really here. I lay there staring out the window for a long time. Finally, I drifted off to sleep.

I slept until the following morning. As I eased myself into a sitting position I groaned in pain. The clock next to my bed said 7:35. Red heard my movements and came over next to me. "Easy boy," I said, "my ribs are still very sore."

The old man heard the commotion and knocked on my door. "Come in," I said. He opened the door and greeted me with a smile.

"How are you this morning?' he asked warmly.

"Better," I answered, "still sore, but better."

"Good, good," he replied.

Red jumped off the bed and walked over to him. "Hi, boy, would you like to go out?" Red ran and barked at the door. "I think he's taken quite a liking to me," tThe old man commented. He let Red out and came back to my room. "Do you need help getting up?" he asked.

"No, I don't think so. I'm going to try it on my own this morning," I answered. As I hung my legs over the side of the bed I groaned in pain. Charlie walked towards me. "I'm okay,

I'm okay," I said pushing up with my arms. I stood up all by myself for the first time in nearly a week.

"Bravo, Bravo!" Charlie bellowed, clapping his hands. I smiled at this curious old man.

"Breakfast will be on the table in five minutes. Oh what a glorious morning!" he shouted in his jovial deep voice as he disappeared into the kitchen.

I washed up and returned to the table. Coffee and muffins sat on the table. Charlie pulled my chair out and I sat down. He sat across from me, smiled and bowed his head.

"Dear Heavenly Father, thank you for a new and glorious day. Thank you for the breath of life and all the wondrous possibilities that lay before us this new day. And Lord we thank you for the food that is before us. I thank you for my new friend Ryan, and we pray for his speedy recovery. And thank you Lord, for the problems in our lives, for I know they are your special gifts in disguise. We thank you for your love and compassion, your wisdom and kindness, your truth and your understanding. Lord, we thank you for all these blessings, in Jesus name. Amen."

I picked up my cup of coffee. Why, I wondered, would anyone be thankful for their problems? And how could our problems be considered gifts from God? I didn't get it. As Charlie sipped his coffee he smiled at me. I forced a smile back. Again, I couldn't get over how Charlie resembled the old man in my dreams. It left me feeling uneasy.

"Ryan, I need to go to town to pick up some supplies. It'll take me several hours. Will you be okay here alone?" he asked. "I'll be fine Charlie," I answered. "Good, good," he answered, taking our dishes to the kitchen. He poured me another cup of coffee. "It's a beautiful day to sit on the porch," he said. "Now make your self at home," he said as he walked out the door.

I heard him start a vehicle. I slowly walked over to the screen door and looked out. Charlie waved from his truck as he backed around. Then down the road he went. The smells of the woods were invigorating and the sun already was taking the morning chill away.

As I sipped my coffee, curiosity was getting the best of me. I slowly examined my surroundings. Books were everywhere, and except for a few pictures, they were his only possessions. Though still in pain, I was feeling the best since I arrived here. I slowly got up and walked over to the shelves of books. There had to be hundreds and hundreds of books.

Books on religion, philosophy, and biographies—there were self help books and books on meditation. There were shelves and shelves of books, and stacks of books on tables scattered around the room. I wondered if Charlie possibly had read all these books. "Red, he is either crazier than me, or a very wise man," I joked. Since I was in his home, I was hoping for the wise scenario. Then I noticed a book sitting on a shelf in the corner by itself. It was wrapped in soft red cloth. I walked over to it almost as if drawn. It was a thick book. My finger slowly laid the cloth back from it. In front of me lay the most exquisite Bible I had ever seen. The leather cover was beautifully ingrained and its pages were edged in gold. I wanted to hold it, but I dared not touch it. I sensed this was something special to the old man.

The cabin was rustic and simply furnished. I noticed it was exceptionally clean. Except for the stacks of books, everything else was neat and orderly. The floors were worn but spotless.

I walked out onto the porch and sat in one of the rockers. Red lay down beside me. As far as I could see was nothing but woods. The sounds of the birds filled the air as they went about their summer activities. A pair of chipmunks darted about searching for food. The air was filled with the smells of nature. I laid my head back and took a deep breath. It felt good to be outside.

But why was I here I wondered? And what made this place so special, as the doc put it? Oh it was beautiful and serene, but my cloud of despair still hung over me. As I sat there staring through the trees, I realized how hopelessly lost I was. Here I was in my early forties, unhappy with my life, disappointed with where I was with my life, unfulfilled in my work and afraid to commit my love to Sarah. My life had lost its purpose and direction. I wondered what my life would be like when blindness would finally overtake me. The sheer frailty of myself frightened me. All the negative feeling and hopelessness I was trying to escape were here all around me. Would I ever find peace?

Though I was thankful to be alive, part of me wished the thugs who had beaten me had killed me. I was tired, tired of pretending to be someone I wasn't, tired of dreams that wouldn't come true, and tired of being afraid. And the thought of losing my sight left me petrified.

Out here there was no one to impress, no one to put up a brave front for, no one at all. I emotionally broke down and cried. I felt like a child stuck in a grown man's body.

While I sat alone drowning in a pool of self pity, I seriously questioned the truth of any of it. Death didn't seem like such an irrational solution. I was tired, very tired and just wanted the turmoil to end.

A loud bang jolted me out of my despairing thoughts. A stiff breeze suddenly blew and I noticed a flower pot broken on the porch. Apparently it had blown off the window sill. Then I realized how depressed my thought had made me. God, I thought, what am I dong here? Here I was amidst natures finest with beauty and tranquility surrounding me and yet I couldn't feel it. I decided to take a little walk hoping the exercise would help chase the blues away.

As my steps fell into a slow progressive pace, my mind began to wander, well, more like someone else's thought trying to force their way into my mind. I suddenly stopped and looked into the sky. My eyes were greeted with a beautiful sea of blue. I suddenly felt a deep sense of shame, shame for all my self pity and despair. "Dear God, please help me, please," I prayed. A voice seemed to talk to me, though there was no sound. An image of the past was dragged across my thoughts. I suddenly realized the fullness of the old man's kindness and compassion. Oh, I had thanked him, but was it truly from my heart? I had become so filled with my own hopeless situation there wasn't much room for love and gratitude.

And I was being shown another side of this old man. I knew little of him, and there was certainly an air of mystique that surrounded him. Here was an old man who seemed totally grateful. Because of his few possessions, most men would think him poor, but he seemed so happy and at peace.

As I walked back to the cabin, I realized there was only one thing I could do. I hadn't come all this way to feel the way I was feeling. It was time for the old man and me to have a talk.

CHAPTER 4

That afternoon the old man invited me out to the porch with him. We both sat down and rocked back and forth. Charlie had been asking different things about me since my arrival, but whenever he asked why I had come to Montana, I wasn't sure how to answer. I did not dare be totally honest for fear of him thinking I was crazy, but there were too many coincidences to ignore. I looked over at him.

His eyes were closed, his lips moving, but not making a sound. He gently rocked back and forth. Slowly he opened his eyes and turned towards me. Noticing my stare he chuckled. "Oh, I was just thanking the Lord for such a beautiful day. Oh, hallelujah!" he chimed.

"The fresh air does feel good," I commented.

He instructed me to close my eyes and take slow deep breaths. "Now, thank God for the clean air filling your lungs. Give thanks for the very essence of life." After several minutes, I did start to feel better, as if I was breathing in new life. "Good, good, Ryan," Charlie said. "I can already see on your face that the power of thankfulness is working in you." I looked at him puzzled. He smiled. "You're wondering what I'm talking about, aren't you?" he asked. I shook my head, yes. "Ryan," he said slowly, "the act of giving thanks is such a powerful force, one that is too lacking in this day and age. You know, people have more than ever before, and yet are not thankful. They lost the meaning and significance of being thankful. And thus no matter how much they have, it is never enough. They are never

29

satisfied. Oh, just a little more and I'll be happy, they say." He shook his head. "What foolish thoughts fill their minds?"

I listened intently to every word, as if drawn to them. He looked at me over his glasses. "Don't you feel better now than you did earlier? At this moment hasn't the power of giving thanks to God eased your depressing thoughts in your mind?" I stopped for a second and realized what he was saying was true. Then I looked at him and asked, "How did you know what I was thinking and feeling earlier?" He smiled at me and said, "That's not important now." Then he continued.

"Ryan, so many people spend their whole lives chasing an illusion of happiness. Oh, they think money, cars, big houses, all the material trappings of our world will bring them happiness, and yet they acquire all these things in abundance and at the end of their lives happiness, joy, and fulfillment has eluded them. How ironic that the secret to acquiring the joy they sought lived in their hearts in the love of God. They're like hamsters running in that metal wheel, forever running, but never really getting anywhere. They get caught in a cycle of greed and want that they never escape from. How sad."

I knew only too well what he was talking about. Despite my good nature and struggles to improve myself, I too, had spent much time on that metal wheel. I felt like one of those people, for I had quickly lost my appreciation of life. Oh, I had moments over the years of appreciation and gratitude for my blessings, but it never lasted. I too, had been chasing the illusion.

"Charlie," I said, "why are people like that? Why are we so ungrateful?" He stared straight ahead for a moment, and then he turned towards me.

"Why, you ask? It is because they have lost their connection to their true self, their spirit, and God. They get caught up in all the trappings of modern society and soon their entire self worth, the way in which they measure value in their life, is tied to their material wealth. When they have abundance they become egotistical, selfish and arrogant. When they have too little, they become depressed, mean and cynical. And like crabs in a pot when they are on the bottom they try to drag everyone else down with them. In this kind of life there is no room for love. All they are concerned with is what they haven't got and why." The old man just shook his head. "And what's even sadder," he added, "is that they raise their children with this attitude so they can become cold and selfish, too. Growing up they're lucky to ever get a glimpse of the true magnificence and power of love, Gods love.

I could see the sadness in Charlie's eyes. "You know, Ryan," he said, "our children deserve so much better than that." I nodded in agreement.

Charlie got up and walked into the cabin. "I'll be back," he said. I sat there still feeling the impact of his words. Something was very different when Charlie spoke. Right now I couldn't put my finger on it, but I was mesmerized every time he spoke. There was a genuine love and compassion that flowed from this old man that could not be resisted.

Maybe I didn't notice it before because of the physical anguish I was in, but I was healing and my mental acuity was back. My senses to my surroundings were no longer a blur. Something was truly unique and special about Charlie. Maybe his talk made me realize how much I already was indebted to this old man who had welcomed me into his home and had taken on the responsibility of nursing me back to health. I felt ashamed, for at first I was suspect of his caring and kindness. Was this the attitude that the eighties and nineties had brought us to?

The opening of the screen door jolted me out of my thoughts. As I looked at Charlie he smiled at me. As he sat next to me, I noticed he had a Bible in his hands. He turned towards me looking out over his glasses. "Ryan, I know you have many questions, which I will answer in time, but fore now, I only want you to take each day one day at a time. And I ask you to remember that there are no coincidences in life. Everything and everyone who touches our lives has a meaning and a purpose.

One of the secrets of life is opening your heart and mind to this truth.

"Since you have arrived, I have paid close attention to you. I can sense the turmoil and despair that rages inside you. I know that your life is in crises and that your very belief and faith in God is in grave doubt."

My mouth dropped open and I just stared at him. "How," I finally muttered, "how do you know? How can you know what's inside of me, how?" I barked. I was starting to feel uneasy. Could he really know how lost and terrified I was? Then, softly and gently he responded.

"Son, it's not important that you know how I know, just remember that our lives haven't crossed by coincidence, but by divine intervention." He smiled at me and put his hands on mine. I've been helping lost souls for half of my life, and you're in need of help, aren't you?"

"Maybe I am," I answered, but I really don't feel like discussing it now." I just wasn't in the mood to spill my guts to the old man. I wasn't ready to acknowledge how much my life was a failure. I lowered my head into my hands.

"Oh, that's okay. Ryan," he said, patting my shoulder. "When you're ready, I'll be here." His kindness and understanding touched me. I sensed that the old man, though a complete stranger, did truly care about me. I felt bad for being so defensive towards him.

"I read from this everyday," he continued, showing me his Bible. I looked up as he spoke. "It brings such joy to my heart. Do you mind if we read a little?" he asked.

"It's okay with me." I answered. He opened his Bible.

As he read I tried to concentrate on his words, but thoughts of my own sad situation interfered. At the end of the page he closed his book and said, "Let us pray." I listened as he gave thanks to the Lord for all his blessings. And as he continued, my heart was pulled by his words. His prayer was that of a common man communicating with God. He even thanked Him for his problems, too! He prayed for the people he knew that needed God's divine help, and then he prayed for me. My emotions stirred as the words of this prayer poured forth. It was as if the old man had crawled inside my soul, for the essence of his words were my cry for help.

As we said "Amen," wiping the tears that ran down my face, a sense of comfort enveloped me. When he finished, he looked up at me. "Ryan" he said gently, "everything you need to know to live a fulfilling and joyful life is here in the Bible." He got up and walked inside.

I laid my head back in the chair and felt the warmth of the afternoon sun. A gentle breeze brushed my face. It felt good to relax. I soon dozed off. Again I dreamed of standing by the cliff with Red. The ground we stood on started to crumble and we began to fall. This time there was no old man to save us, just a voice saying, "Have faith and believe in me, for I am always with you. Reach out for me," the voice said, fading as we fell farther into the abyss.

The sense of falling jerked me awake. I groaned in pain from the sudden movement. Charlie came to the door. "Are you okay, son?" he asked.

"Yes, just another dream. Why am I having all these dreams all of a sudden," I moaned. He just smiled and went back to whatever he was doing.

The old rocker creaked as I climbed out of it. I decided to take a little walk and shake the cobwebs in my head loose. Red ran a short distance ahead of me. After walking a hundred yards or so, I sat down on a stump next to a huge oak tree. I marveled at the size of the tree. Its truck was approximately six feet around and it had to be close to two hundred feet tall. I wondered how many hundreds of years this old giant had been watching over the forest.

As I sat there lost in solitude, I lost myself in my thoughts. What was happening to me and where was I? Was it, as Charlie said, that I was here with him through divine intervention? There was a strange and mystical presence to this place, a sense of fear ran through me too, but strangely, underlying my fear was a feeling of comfort, of being safe. Oh, I knew it didn't make sense, but it was how I felt.

Red barked as he ran chasing a squirrel through the under brush. At least he was enjoying himself. I called out his name as I got up to start back. Then all of a sudden, as if he appeared out of thin air, there was the old man. He startled me so that I nearly lost my balance. "I'm sorry, Ryan," he calmly said, "I didn't mean to startle you."

"How did you just appear like you do?" I asked. No reply, just that big warm smile of his.

"Dinner is about ready, so I decided to come after you," he said.

"Why, thank you," I replied. "Red and I were just starting back." We walked the rest of the way in silence. I was still bewildered by his sudden appearance.

When we reached the cabin, a lady came walking out the back door. "Betsy, Betsy!" Charlie bellowed. "How are you this beautiful fine day?"

"Oh just terrific," she replied.

Charlie introduced me and we exchanged greetings. "So, you're the gentleman Charlie's taking care of," she said. "How are you doing?" she asked.

"Oh, I'm still a little sore, but I'm feeling better every day."

"Good, good," she replied. "You're in wonderful hands," she said, smiling at Charlie. "Oh, I left you some fresh baked bread to go with your dinner."

"Oh, you're an angel, Betsy," Charlie teased. "She bakes the best bread you've ever tasted, Ryan," he said smiling. "Oh, you're in for a treat!" his eyes wide with delight.

Betsy was a jolly, energetic lady who appeared to be in her fifties. Her black hair was streaked with grey. She chatted with us for a while and then said she had to be going. We said our goodbyes and watched her drive off.

Charlie informed me that Betsy lived about a half mile down the road and stopped by once a week to chat and bring baked goods. "She is a wonderful cook," Charlie said, "and a wonderful lady. Her husband died a few years ago from cancer. Her visits always brighten my day," he added.

As I sat down to dinner, Charlie brought in Betsy's bread. It was still warm and its aroma filled the room. The old man carefully sliced several pieces. He delighted in the anticipation of his first taste. I watched as he closed his eyes savoring his first bite. I couldn't help but laugh. He opened his eyes and smiled at me. "Go ahead," he gestured "see what you think." The bread was as delicious as Charlie had said. We laughed as we ate out meal.

I hadn't laughed in weeks. I had almost forgotten how good it felt. Here in these humble surroundings this kind and gentle man had made me feel both wanted and loved. It was an enjoyable evening.

CHAPTER 5

Iwas awakened the following morning by Charlie's whistling and singing. I noticed as I got out of bed that the sharpness of the pain in my ribs had lessened. Moving was getting easier and less painful. As I opened the bedroom door, Red cheerfully greeted me. I walked over to the back door and let him out. As I turned to walk to the bathroom, Charlie greeted me. "Good morning, friend!" his booming voice filled the cabin.

"Morning," I replied.

"And how are you on this beautiful day?" he chimed. "Thankful, oh yes, be thankful!" he bellowed.

"I am," I replied half-heartedly as I closed the bathroom door. I washed my face and brushed my teeth. When I looked in the mirror I thought to myself, who is this old man? I was still struggling between acceptance and resistance. Why was he so happy? I wondered…He lived alone and except for a bunch of books and his old truck, what did he have? I stared in the mirror but no answer came. Was it all because of his belief in God? I believed in God, or so I thought I did and my life was a total mess. What was I doing wrong? Could I learn the answers I desperately sought from this kind old gentleman? Somewhere deep inside I knew I need not travel any further.

I barely recognized the face staring back at me. I had now been gone from home for over two weeks and hadn't shaved since I left. The stitches in the side of my head looked awful. I was glad they'd soon be out. While I was feeling better, I still looked pretty ragged.

As I walked to the table, Charlie greeted me with a smile. "Ah, yes, splendid! Yes, indeed, splendid!" he bellowed.

"What is?" I asked as I sat down.

"You," he answered. "I can see you're getting around much better. How are your ribs feeling?" he questioned.

"They're still sore, Charlie," I answered, "but the pain isn't nearly as bad."

"Good, good" he replied, "Oh, by the way, Doc will be by this morning to take out those stitches."

"I'm glad," I answered. "They look awful."

After breakfast a knock came on the door. "Come in, come in," Charlie said cheerfully. It was Doc.

"How's my patient doing?" he asked.

"Still a little sore, but better."

"Good, good," he replied.

Charlie poured a cup of coffee for his old friend and we chatted for awhile. I liked Doc. He was warm and friendly and funny. "Do you always make house calls?" I asked.

"Oh, I do quite a bit out here," he answered. "People like to be treated in the comfort of their homes," he continued. "I don't like being cramped in an old office anyhow," he commented.

He chatted with Charlie as he removed my stitches. Before I knew it, he was finished. I thanked him and asked how much I owed. "Not a dime," he cheerfully answered. "Charlie took care of my fee so don't worry about it." He packed his medical bag, wished us well, and said goodbye.

We watched him drive off. "Charlie, he's such a nice man, and a terrific doctor. I know a few doctors who could learn a lot from old Pete," I said.

"I know, Ryan, I know."

I pleaded with Charlie to allow me to pay him something for the Doc's care, but he would have none of that. "Doc and I have an arrangement," he said.

He looked out over his glasses and smiled. "I'll tell you how in time."

He informed me he had errands to run and would be gone for several hours. Again he told me to make myself at home. "Pick out a book for yourself," he said. A short while later he drove off in his old truck. I couldn't help but chuckle watching him drive off whistling and singing. If he weren't such a Godly man, I would swear he was on drugs.

I walked back in the cabin and looked through his books again. I was amazed at the wealth of knowledge in his collection. Religion, philosophy, inspirational books on all the greats filled the room.

As I looked over his collection, I pulled out one book after another. Now how was I to pick just one book from this enormous collection? After fifteen minutes or so I pulled out a small paperback book. As I leafed through it's pages, I realized it was a book of daily readings. This isn't what I want I thought, it's not even a story. But oddly I couldn't put it down. I browsed some more, keeping the small paperback under my arm. Finally, not understanding why, I decided to keep this maroon little book. As I carried it to my room, I read the title: *My Utmost for His Highest* by Oswald Chambers. Odd title I thought, and who was Oswald Chambers? I placed it down on the stand by the bed. I knew I could learn from this wise and caring old man, but what? And I still knew nothing about him, except he was special. I decided to try the half mile walk to Betsy's. Maybe she could shed some light on this mysterious man.

I wrote a note to Charlie in case he got home before me and I placed it on the table. I told Red we were taking a walk and he exuberantly ran for the back door. As we walked, I was in awe of the peace and tranquility that surrounded us. I wondered what insights Betsy would share about Charlie. I only hoped she would be home.

We passed no other houses or people on our way to Betsy's. At last I could make out a house in the distance. That has to be it, I told Red. Then I recognized her car in the driveway. Her house was small with plants and flowers all around. A wind chime hung on the front porch, playing in the breeze.

I knocked on the door several times, but no one answered. I walked around back. No one seemed to be around. Red barked and ran down in the woods. Then I heard her bubbly voice. "Back here!" she yelled, waving her arms in the air. I waved back and walked towards her. "Good day to you," she said smiling. "I'm so happy to see you. Where's Charlie?" she asked.

"Oh, he had some errands to run, so we thought we'd come for a visit."

"Wonderful, wonderful!" she said gleefully. "It will give us a chance to talk."

She placed the last of the mushrooms she had picked in a pail. "You're just in time for lunch," she said. "Please say you'll stay."

I said I would be happy to. On the walk back to the house, she shared memories of her beloved Frank, her late husband. "We so loved this place," she continued. "A little piece of heaven on earth." I couldn't help but notice how her face would light up whenever she spoke of her husband.

"You must have loved him very much," I said.

"Oh, I still do, Ryan. He's a part of me and always will be," she said patting her heart. "Come in, come in," she said. "You, too Red." She led us to the kitchen and motioned for me to sit down. Her home was beautifully decorated, yet quaint. The kitchen was clean and neat as a pin. I instantly felt welcomed.

"Are you married, Ryan?" she asked. As she washed the mushrooms she had just picked.

"No, I'm divorced," I replied."

Any children?" she asked.

"Yes, I have a wonderful son," I answered. "He stays with his mom during the summer. He's 10 years old and his name is Brent." I reached for my wallet to show her a picture, but I didn't have it with me. "

"What is that heavenly smell?" I asked.

"Oh, that's our lunch," she replied. "Fresh made vegetable soup and bread." She sliced some of the mushrooms and added them to the soup. "Lunch will be ready shortly," she said. "I hope you're hungry." I was, my appetite had returned since the beating.

Betsy set the table and dished out her soup. She said grace and we proceeded to enjoy a delicious meal. I complimented her on her cooking expertise which she accepted very modestly.

"Is there a special someone in your life, Ryan?" she asked me. I thought of Sarah and wondered how she was doing. By now she had to have read the letter I left her. I wasn't sure how to answer. Betsy noticed my silence. "I'm sorry, I don't mean to pry," she said sincerely. "You just seem like such a nice young man, I just assumed there was someone."

"That's okay." I replied. "I do have a very special lady in my life. I just wonder if she'll still be there when I get home." Betsy looked at me questioning my comment, but didn't pry.

We chatted some more about her late husband and her children. Also I shared with her where I lived and some details about my divorce.

After lunch she invited me out on her deck for some tea. There were pots of flowers placed around the deck. On one end was lattice, filled with flowering vines. I watched as several humming birds darted back and forth filling themselves with the sweet nectar of the splendid blooms.

"It is so beautiful out here," I commented.

"Yes it is," she replied. "I thank God every day for the blessing of these woods."

"Charlie's Woods, right?" I said with a chuckle.

"Why, yes," she answered, somewhat surprised. "You know about Charlie's Woods?" she asked.

"No, I don't," I replied. "It's just that you and Doc refer to this place as Charlie's Woods. Doc told me this is a very specials place, Betsy."

"Oh, it is Ryan, it really is. I'll stay here until I die," she said happily.

"Don't you ever get lonely living out here?" I asked.

"Oh, my no," she responded. "I love the peace and solitude. I feel close to God out here. I've lived here now close to forty years," she continued. "I have friends in town I visit, and they visit me from time to time, and Charlie, well, I couldn't have a nicer or friendlier neighbor. I'm truly content here," she added.

"Charlie told me about you being attacked. What a shame," she said. "Hardly anything ever happens like that around here, so when it does, it's shocking." I explained what had happened the best that I could, and what my plans were. "Oh, I bet your plans are all ruined," she said sympathetically.

"Not really," I replied. "I had no concrete plans. I just had this compelling need to come out here in search of something. I'm not sure what. And now I'm in Charlie's Woods. Why does everyone call this place Charlie's Woods, anyhow? I can't imagine he owns all this," I said.

"Oh," she said, "but he does, as far as you can see." My mouth dropped open in shock. Betsy laughed at my expression.

"I don't understand," I gasped, "he lives so modestly and drives that old truck. I thought all his worldly possessions were his books. How much land does he own?" I asked. Betsy looked at me and smiled. "Nearly five thousand acres," she answered. I shook my head in disbelief. "See, Ryan. Money no longer matters to Charlie. In fact, upon his death, this land goes to the state of Montana on the condition that it's preserved in its natural pristine state as God created it. He keeps enough money to take care of his needs, the rest he gives away."

I sat there totally dumbfounded. "Betsy, I don't understand any of this. Please tell me about Charlie. I really need to know."

She poured us some more tea and handed me a plate of cookies. "Well, let me start at the beginning," she said. "Charlie grew up in New York City. His parents were poor immigrants from Germany. They worked hard and sent Charlie to the best schools. In fact he went to Harvard, top of his class. He went to

41

work on Wall Street and made a fortune." I sat there stunned at the story that was unfolding before me.

"What happened?" I asked hungry to hear more.

"Well, Charlie fell in love, got married and two years later their daughter was born."

"Where are they now?" I asked.

"Be patient," Betsy teased, pointing her finger at me. Then she continued. "They had all the trappings of material life. Money, cars, several homes, they had it all. Charlie adored his wife and daughter. They seemed like the perfect family.

"Shortly after Beth turned twelve, that's Charlie's daughter, her mother and her were coming home from a play. They were only a few miles from home, when a drunk driver crossed the road and crashed head on into their car. Charlie's wife was killed instantly and Beth was critically injured, and in a coma.

"Charlie left his prestigious job to be with his daughter. He was by her side day and night for six agonizing months."

"What happened?" I asked, shocked by the story she was telling.

"His beloved daughter died. Charlie was devastated. He went into a destructive and downward spiral. He no longer paid attention to his personal or business affairs. He drank too much and became a recluse. To look at him, you would've thought him a bum, not a rich and powerful man. He had lost all appreciation for life.

"One night late in the evening, he found himself wandering around the Brooklyn Bridge. He decided he had suffered enough. He wanted to be with his wife and little girl. He was going to end his life. See, Ryan, he lost something even more precious, his faith in God."

"Because of the accident," I said softly.

"Yes, Ryan," Betsy answered. "He had prayed everyday of those six months his Beth lay in a coma. And still she died. He became so angry with God and his heart filled with hate until that hate sucked every last bit of life from him."

"What stopped him from jumping?" I pressed.

"Well, as Charlie tells it, he was ready to jump when the squealing of tires distracted him for just a second. The car flipped several times, finally stopping on its roof less than fifty yards from him.

"He heard a little girl cry out for help. He jumped off the bridge and ran to the car. The little girl was bleeding and crying and trapped. Charlie ran to the driver's side of the car to check the driver. The driver's face was turned towards him, but he was motionless—killed instantly. As he was checking the driver, Charlie was filled with rage for this was the man who had killed his wife and daughter. He let out an awful scream, his hate exploding forth. Yes, he even thought for a second of leaving. Why should I save your girl, he screamed? But the little girl's cries brought Charlie out of his rage. He couldn't leave her.

"He went around to her side of the car and lay on his stomach, reached through the broken window and held her hand. Slowly, her crying lessened as Charlie kept telling her she would be okay. He found himself praying for God to save this little girl. Suddenly a bright light appeared over the car. A figure stood in the center of this bright pulsating light. The figure called out to Charlie, 'I am with her as I am with you. Be not afraid. She will be alright.' Charlie at first doubted his eyes and ears for he had been drinking. But then the light hovered over him. A feeling of warmth and love enveloped him. Never had he ever experienced such a pure and giving love. 'Go home, for I have a work for you to do. I will look after the girl.' Charlie got up and headed for home as if in a trance. He turned back to see the ambulance pull up to the crash. The light that hovered over the car faded away.

"That night Charlie tossed and turned, not able to get the vision he had witnessed out of his mind. The next morning as he watched the news, he learned that the little girl was only slightly injured and the driver dead at the scene. The report confirmed the driver's identity.

"The next night as he slept, the vision returned. He doesn't know if it was a dream or real. He does know these visions saved his life. As the bright light appeared, he noticed there were three figures in the light. Two of them stepped forward out of the light. It was his wife and daughter. He sat up in bed reaching for them and calling their names. They told him they were fine and that they loved him. They told him not to worry and that they would see him again, but not now. "Listen to him," they said, as they stepped back into the light, into his outstretched arms. Then the light slowly faded away. When he awoke he was crying, but a feeling of peace and love filled his heart for the first time since their death."

I could hardy believe what I was hearing. "But how did he wind up here?" I asked Betsy. "What can he do out here in the middle of nowhere?"

Betsy looked at me and smiled. "The Lord's work," she said.

"How?" I quickly asked.

"In another vision he was told "to live in harmony with nature and to love and teach those I send to you. To love those souls who were lost and floundering on the edge of life."

A strange sensation started to go through me. "But why Montana, Betsy, why here? Tell me, I have to know," I blurted out.

"Well," she continued, "several weeks went by and Charlie was trying to make sense of it all. He had regained his thirst for life and was driven by the visions he had witnessed, but he was puzzled by the visions. Who would he be helping and how? And living in harmony with nature really confused him, since he had lived in New York City all his life.

"Then one day while reading the newspaper, he noticed a large add in the real estate section: "For Sale 5000 Acres of beautiful pristine wilderness, a piece of heaven on earth." Charlie took it as a message from God. He contacted the owners, got his business affairs in order, flew out to Montana and bought it on the spot."

I sat there shaking my head in disbelief. I had a new understanding and affection for this kind old gentleman, and then it hit me like a brick. I just stared at Betsy as I started trembling. She smiled and softly said. "You were chosen to come here, Ryan, you know that now, don't you?"

I could barely force my words out. "But, why Betsy? Why me?" I said nearly choking on the words.

My heart was pounding and my mind racing. Now I understood the pull to come to Montana, but what was going to happen to me? Betsy noticed my anxiety.

"Ryan, don't be nervous or afraid," she said gently. "I've seen this before."

"What?" I snapped.

"Oh, the other people that have come through Charlie's Woods." Her voice was calm and caring. "Some set of circumstances always leads Charlie to them."

"What happens to them Betsy? Tell me." I was frantic now.

"All I can tell you, Ryan, is that their lives are forever changed. Be thankful, Ryan, for you have been blessed by coming here."

I got up out of my chair. "I've gotta talk to Charlie, Betsy," I said. I felt as if I was going to throw up. I thanked her for her hospitality, but I need to go. I walked out her lane quickly. I would have run if I could. She called after me. "Ryan, remember, God loves you!"

My walk back was much quicker. I was too numb to sense any pain. This was all too weird and I was truly shaken by her story. My mind was racing. What did she mean, I was chosen? Chosen for what? I wasn't anybody special. I felt as if I was being guided by forces I had no control over. Any peace that I had been feeling was gone. I was frightened and part of me wanted to run away from here.

As I neared Charlie's cabin, my ribs started to ache. I got to the porch and collapsed in one of the rocking chairs trying to catch my breath. I was still trembling.

Charlie's Woods

What was going on here? Why would I of all people be chosen to come here? Was this for real or was I stuck in some never ending nightmare?

I struggled to calm myself but was filled with too much fear and anxiety. I needed some answers and I needed them now. Tonight I would get them.

CHAPTER 6

Charlie pulled in the driveway about an hour later. I was still lost in a sea of thoughts. "Hello, my friend, "he said, in his cheery voice. "Are you enjoying this is beautiful afternoon?" he asked with a big smile on his face.

"I guess so," I replied half heartedly. I just wanted to sit him down and share with him what Betsy shared with me earlier. I had so many questions that needed answers.

The old man noticed the mood I was in. "Are you okay, Ryan?" he asked, with concern in his voice. "You seem troubled, son," he said as he sat down next to me.

"I'm not sure of anything, Charlie," I replied.

"Did something happen while I was gone?" he inquired.

I nodded my head. "Yes, it did, Charlie. Red and I paid Betsy a visit. I thought the walk would do me good. No that's not true Charlie, I went there to find out about you," I confessed.

"Oh," he said. "I'm sure she was delighted to see you," he said. "She doesn't entertain folks very often. And how was your visit?" he asked, the tone in his voice softening.

"It was interesting," I answered. "We enjoyed a wonderful lunch together and had quite a chat," I continued.

"I see," he replied, looking over his glasses at me as if in thought.

My anxiety was exploding inside of me as I relived her words in my thoughts. "Charlie, I don't understand what's going on here, the things Betsy told me." I was starting to tremble.

He motioned for me to be silent.

"Ryan, I know," he said. "I know."

"But," I started.

"Sh-h-h!" he said. "Please, son, be patient a little longer. We'll talk after dinner, I promise," he said, looking into my eyes with compassion and understanding. He got up and head-ed for the door, shaking his head. I heard him mumble as he went inside, "That Betsy, she does go on."

He reappeared a good while later, informing me that dinner was started. I got up and went in the house and set the table. As I set the plates and silverware, I could feel Charlie's eyes upon me. The power of his presence could be overwhelming. My anxiety had subsided some, but I was still filled with so many questions about this old man and this place called Charlie's Woods. I didn't know how I would ever sit down to eat, but I knew I had to force myself. The old man's meals were never fancy, but always delicious. The smell of the chicken baking stirred my appetite. When dinner was ready, he said grace and we began our meal in silence. Every now and then he'd look up at me and smile. The silence was driving me crazy. "Charlie," I finally said, breaking the silence, "we really need to talk." He finished what he was chewing.

"I know," he replied, looking out over those glasses of his. "After dinner, we have much work to do. Now try to enjoy your dinner," he said.

Through the rest of our meal I kept my eyes on Charlie. He seemed deep in thought, so I kept my mouth shut. We cleaned up from dinner and Charlie asked me to start a fire, since the evening air was cool. As I placed the kindling and wood in the fireplace, I kept thinking about what this special man would discuss this evening.

Once I had the fire going, I went out and brought in a few more pieces of wood and then stacked them in his wood box. Charlie had two glasses in his hand. "Would you join me in having a drink?" he asked. Now I warn you, this has a little kick to it.

"What is it?" I inquired.

"Oh Ryan, it's a very special tea that I only make for special occasions." I agreed to join him. I sorely needed something to calm my nerves. As he filled our glasses with the golden liquid, a sweet fragrance filled my senses. He held his glass close to his nose and inhaled the sweet fragrance. The fragrance was heavenly and had an immediate soothing and calming effect, almost intoxicating. He raised his glass to mine. "To friendship and love." I took a sip of the mysterious drink. "Charlie, this is truly delicious and refreshing!" I said. "What is it?"

"Oh, it's a very special blend of teas and herbs that a wise old friend introduced me to. The ingredients are very rare, so I only make it on special occasions."

We both sat down by the fire. The old man sat there savoring the simple pleasure of fine drink, so I tried doing the same. But I needed answers. The wait was excruciating.

After what seemed an eternity, he sat his glass down. I did likewise. He turned his chair more towards me. "Ryan, he said, with seriousness in his voice. I know you have many questions, even more so after today. If your heart is open and you truly trust in me, I will help you find the answers."

"But, how, how can you?" I blurted out. The old man looked at me with annoyance for my interruption. I quickly apologized and allowed him to continue.

"There are so many people today in the world, who like you, are good and decent, but they have lost their way. In an effort to fill the emptiness in their souls, to relieve the pain in their lives, they turn down many paths searching for something. I'm sure you have traveled on some of these same paths, and all eventually lead to destruction, drugs, alcohol, hatred, false pride, jealousy and fear. Many become mean and abusive trying to make themselves feel better at others expense. They lash out, criticize, gossip, lie, anything in an attempt to build their egos, and there self exaggerated importance. They all get so caught up in their own destructive circumstances that they lose their ability to feel love, and compassion and joy." He sat there shaking his head.

"They futilely try to keep building their lives on a foundation of sand instead of one in stone. They create a life of certain failure and eventually spend all the blessed energy of life on hate and blame and envy. Their lives become filled with excuses and they lose the consciousness of accepting responsibility for their choices. Ryan, every one of us has the power of choice. It is one of the true gifts from God, and most dangerous, the total freedom of choice. And yet many still blame God for the emptiness and failure of their lives."

I could identify only too well with the words he had spoken, for they were hitting so close to home. I was one of those lost souls he was talking about.

He got up and stood by the fireplace. "Ryan, they all have so much to be thankful for, including you, but their hearts have been blinded by their unbelief and lack of faith." Now the old man was starting to lose me, and I certainly wasn't feeling any better. In fact, I was feeling ashamed. This wasn't how I was expecting him to make me feel.

He walked over and sat down. "Ryan, when we pray to God, we should always offer prayers of thanks for He is all we ever need. Too often when people pray, they're always asking for something, and when the prayers aren't answered in the way they expect, then God isn't real, God doesn't care, they'll even say He's an unloving God."

I could see the sadness in Charlie's eyes. He was quiet for a moment and I dared not say a word. I was filled with mixed emotions. I so much respected and was in awe of this wonderful old man, but I knew in my heart that God had not answered my prayers. How could I tell him that? I sat staring into the fire when he resumed speaking.

"Ryan, I am here to help you with your rebirth, a new life, if you will allow me. I can feel the unbelief in your heart, and the despair in your soul. Let us take a minute to pray. Will you lead us in prayer?" he asked calmly. I bowed my head, but felt so unsure of what to say in the presence of such a wise and Godly man. I suddenly and unexplainably became filled with a volatile mix of emotions. He would see through me if I uttered words, and I didn't share his unshakable faith in God. The silence became unbearable, and the words wouldn't come. Finally, I looked up at him and whispered, "I can't, I don't know why, I just can't." He reached over to touch my hands, and I pulled away. I didn't understand why I did. I did know the shame and inadequacy I was feeling could no longer be contained. I suddenly felt like a volcano ready to erupt. All my emotions were racing out of control. I was suddenly filled with anger and didn't know why. I couldn't even look at the old man.

"Ryan," he said, just talk to God. He will listen. Unburden your heart to Him. I just exploded, jumping out of my chair.

"Maybe he listens to you," I shouted. "But how could he care about me? And you know what? I don't care about Him either!" I screamed. "Who are you anyway, and why do you even care?" I couldn't control myself. I felt as if I was possessed. Everything that I had been holding in since I left home came flooding out. "My life is a living hell," I yelled. "Is that how God has answered my prayers?" I spewed forth all the misfortunes of my life. The death of my mother as a boy, the abusive years with my stepmother, an unloving father, failed relationships, and insecurities. I was a madman.

"And do you know what the final blessing is that he is giving to me?" I shouted, raising my arms and looking to the heavens. "He's going to allow me to go blind!" I looked at him coldly. "Now tell me how to thank God for all those blessings. You find the words!" I screamed. "Go ahead, tell me what to say!"

He stood there, didn't blink an eye. He quietly listened to my ungratefulness, my rudeness, my anger, and my pain. Why, why, why, Charlie, why, why?" as the tears came flooding forth and I collapsed in his arms. He held me as I broke down, sobbing uncontrollably. "Why, Charlie, why has he deserted me?"

All the pain and anguish of my years flooded out of me in my stream of tears.

As the old giant held me, he quietly whispered, "God always has been with you, son, trust me, trust me. Just let it all out," he said comforting me. He held me for the longest time.

Finally I spoke. "Charlie, I'm so sorry. I feel so ashamed," I whispered.

"Son, it's okay, truly, this was necessary," he replied softly. "This is a good thing, son, trust me." Slowly I calmed down, but I was exhausted. The old man gently hugged me and said, "God loves you and so do I." His words sent a feeling of warmth through me. I could feel the love emanate from him. Finally, I said I was okay and he let me go. I collapsed in the chair, letting out a sigh of relief. I started to apologize again, but Charlie motioned for me to be silent. As I sat there catching my breath, I felt a true sense of relief, like a huge weight had been lifted off my shoulders.

He gently placed his hands on mine. "Ryan, sometimes we need to get to the lowest point in our life, where we feel hopeless, afraid and alone before God will truly allow us to witness His glory. I know," he continued, "forty-two years ago I was where you are now. I know how you feel, for I felt exactly the same anger and hopelessness you feel. For some reason, God chose to turn me around, and I didn't understand at the time either, bur I certainly do now. I'm here to help you, son, will you allow me?" he asked, his voice filled with compassion. I nodded my head, wearily.

"Yes," I said.

CHAPTER 7

Once I had calmed down I realized I had no energy left to hide or pretend. The only thing I could do was bare my soul to this man of God. I knew whatever was going to save me was right here with him. I was just too tired to fight anymore. Quietly and calmly I unburdened my heart to him. Slowly I relived the pain of my past, the anguish and confusion of losing my mother as a boy, the horrific abusive years with my stepmother, the longing to feel the love of a father who didn't know how to show it, the deep rooted insecurities that led me to destructive and failed relationships.

I paused for a moment while the anguish of my past flooded over me one more time. Charlie's expression seemed to echo the pain I was reliving. "Go on, Ryan," he said, his gentle voice assuring me.

"Charlie, everyone around me thinks I have my life in order and that I'm on top of things when in reality, on the inside, I'm a mess. And the older I become, the more doubt and fear fill my life." I said.

"What are you afraid of Ryan?" he asked.

I shook my head. "I'm afraid of never feeling in control of my life, of never feeling secure in love, of never finding peace. My life seems always to be haunted by insecurity and doubt. I'm tired of pretending to be something I'm not and never filling the emptiness that lives deep inside of me. Charlie," I said, looking at him. "I can't live the lie anymore. Nothing about me seems real, my life seems like an illusion with no substance.

I'm just a phony who dreams about big dreams and accomplishes little. Except for my son and Sarah, I hate my life. And even that I've messed up."

The hopelessness I was feeling was overwhelming. My next comment brought sadness to the old man's face. "I don't even know if I believe in God anymore. Why would He allow so much pain and sorrow to surround my life? And the final straw, Charlie, is I found out just before leaving to come to Montana that I have an untreatable eye disease that will eventually leave me blind. Now do you understand why I don't feel thankful or blessed?

"Charlie, what have I done wrong? What is the matter with me? God please help me, Charlie. I can't live like this any longer." He looked at me for a long time before he spoke.

"Son," he interrupted, "you give yourself no credit at all. I've watched you during your stay here. You have an incredible and loving bond with your dog. He hangs on your every word. He saved your life you know. And what about the wonderful and loving relationship you have with your son? You have made many sacrifices in order to give him a loving and secure home. I can tell by the conversations we shared how deep your love is for the boy."

"I know Charlie," I replied, "But I also know that my choices have brought him pain."

"Ryan, Ryan, we all make choices that don't work out as we hoped," he answered. "It takes a loving parent and you possess such a love. But you must know that to possess, to feel such a love, one has to be connected to God. And what about Sarah?" he continued. "She sounds like such a special lady. Do you think she could love you like she does if you were not a very special man?"

"I don't feel special Charlie, and I certainly don't feel worthy of that love." I said desperately.

"Ryan, you are much more special than you realize. You have so many wonderful qualities that you have lost sight of, and despite the tragic events that you have encountered on your journey in life, you have never been alone. God has always been by your side, son, how else can you explain surviving all that you have and still have such a loving and forgiving heart?"

"If you say so, Charlie." I mumbled.

He looked at me with understanding. "Son," he said, "it's not important what I say or think, but what you feel in your heart." He got up out of his chair and motioned for me to sit at the table. He walked over to one of his bookshelves and started searching for something. After several minutes of searching, "Ah, there it is," I heard him say. He walked back to the table with what appeared to be a rolled up scroll. He sat down with the scroll in his hands. "Ryan," he spoke softly, "many years ago when your mother went to heaven, you were a small boy confused and saddened by God's taking her. One day you came across these words that comforted that little boy and through the years have reappeared at different events in your life, always touching you profoundly. Today, right now, their meaning may have clarity as never before."

Handing me the rolled up paper, he said, "I'd like you to have this." I reached out and took it from his hands. The paper was thick and old. He watched me take the ribbon off it and slowly unroll it.

As I began to read the first verse, my hands started to shake. "How could he know?" I thought. "Dear God how could he know?" My eyes became moist as I red the words in front of me.

FOOTPRINTS

One night a man had a dream. He dreamed he was walking along the beach with the Lord. Across the sky flashed scenes from his life. For each scene, he noticed two sets of footprints in the sand; one belonging to him, the other to the Lord.

When the last scene of his life flashed before him, he looked back at the footprints in the sand. He noticed that many times along the path of his life there were only one set of footprints. He also noticed that it happened at the very lowest and saddest times in is life.

This really bothered him and he questioned the Lord about it. "Lord, you said that once I decided to follow you, you'd walk with me all the way. But I have noticed that during the most troublesome times in my life, there was only one set of footprints. I don't understand why when I needed you most, you would leave me.

The Lord replied, "My son, my precious child. I love you and would never leave you. During your times of trial and suffering, when you see only one set of footprints, it was then that I carried you."

The picture of the footprints in the sand had been burned into my memory. Again, the words impacted me as always. My eyes were moist with tears and a feeling of love came over me. The same feeling came over me as it always did when those words would find there way into my troubled life. I closed my eyes and pressed the scroll to my chest, slowly breathing. The old man was right, its message carried a clarity that they hadn't before. All those times I thought he hadn't heard my prayers; He was there by my side all the while. I slowly rolled the scroll up. I looked at this wonderful old man sitting across from me, struggling hard to hold back the tears. "How," I said "How can you know? Oh God in heaven, how can you know?"

His expression was filled with compassion. "Because God loves you," was his reply.

I was in strange territory. I didn't understand how any of this could be real. How could a stranger know so much about me? But I didn't care. I was just thankful he was here.

"Charlie, I don't understand." I said grabbing his hands.

"Soon you will, my son, soon you will."

"You see, Ryan," he continued, "the message in *Footprints in the Sand* was God's quiet voice assuring you that he was watching over you.

"God is always there for us, always, if we will only ask for His divine help. He tries to get our attention in so many ways, but way too often we get so caught up in our problems that we never hear his voice."

"I guess I'm one of those people aren't I," I sadly replied.

He chuckled, "Ryan, remember we are all children of God, and as children we don't always listen as much as we should. That is why God gave us two ears and one mouth. More listening and less talking is crucial in developing and nurturing a sound relationship."

"How do I do that, Charlie?" I asked. "How do I develop a clearer relationship with God.?"

"Ah," he said with a smile. Now you have asked a question for the ages and here in lies your answer," he replied, pushing his Bible towards me. "Please read John 1-1: *In the beginning was the Word of God."*

I turned to the next passage, John 3-16: *For God so loved the world that he gave His only begotten Son, that whoever believes in Him should not parish, but have eternal life.* John 5-24: *Truly, truly I say unto you, He who hears my words and believes in Him who sent Me has eternal life; he does not come into judgment, but has passed from death to life.*

As I looked up the old man's eyes were focused on me. Acts 2-21: My voice steadied as I proceeded. *"And it shall be that whoever calls on the name of the Lord shall be saved.* The words carried a clarity I never carried before. Ephesians 2-8 & 9: *For by grace you have been saved through faith and it is not of your doing, it is the gift of God, not because of works lest any man should boast.* Romans 10-9&10: *Because if you confess with your lips, that Jesus is Lord and believe in your heart that God raised Him from the dead, you will be saved. For man believes with his heart and so is justified and confesses with his lips and so is saved.* Then I turned to the last passage marked, John 14-6: *Jesus said to him, "I am the way, and the truth and the life; no one comes to the Father but by Me.*

When I finished I looked up at the old man with a look of uncertainty of what I just read.

What happened next I will never forget. I heard that voice, "Stay true to the path I've put you on and trust in me for I am with you always." I turned in my chair and searched the room.

"Charlie," I said softly, "Did you hear that?"

The old man looked up at me perplexed.

"The voice, the voice," I repeated. "Did you hear the voice?"

He shook his head and smiled. A strange calmness settled over me. The old man looked at me for the longest time.

"Son," he said putting his hands on the Bible, "this is the voice of God. The passages I had you read were for a purpose. First, believe that the word of God contained in the pages are everything you need to know to live a loving and fulfilling life. His word is truth. Anything else is not of God!" I sat there embracing every word. I don't know how but I grasped an understanding of what he was saying and I hungered for more.

"Now in order for you to have a new life, you must first shed your old life. 'No one comes to the Father but by Me.' " I looked up at the old man, my eyes searching. He smiled at me. "Son, to have a true and deep relationship with God, you must surrender your heart to Jesus Christ and ask him to come into your life."

"But how do I do that?" I asked. "What words do I say?"

"There are no set words, no clever phrases or even noble sayings, Ryan. Just let the words pour from your heart for they will be sure and true. Be humble, but not afraid when you ask Jesus into you life. Confess your past so that it may be tossed away and be open to the new life to come."

He then informed me he was retiring for the evening.

"But Charlie," I protested. "I need you here."

He stopped at his bedroom door and turned around. "Ryan," he said with conviction in his voice. "For this you do not need me. Confess from your heart and have faith. I leave you in much more capable hands than mine. You'll do just fine." At that he smiled, turned and walked into his room and shut his door. I sat there not sure what to do next. Why would he leave me here like this? Slowly my eyes were drawn to the portrait above the fireplace. As my eyes settled on the crucifixion, a well of emotions started to build up inside me. Then as if moved by some invisible force, I climbed out of my chair, walked over to the fireplace and fell to my knees. I bowed my head still not sure of what to pray and then the words and emotions just flowed forth. I confessed to God what a mess I had made of my life. As my past poured out of me the feelings became almost overwhelming. I was in tears, sobbing out my cynicism and ingratitude, my self pity and lack of faith. Everything of my past came flooding out. I prayed to God to rid myself of all the pain and despair. I begged Jesus to come into my heart and save me from myself. Finally, there was nothing left to come out.

I sat back on the floor exhausted from the experience. It took several minutes to regain my composure and then I noticed a strange sensation flowing through me, a sense of cleansing. All the old dirt was being washed away. There was an inner peace that I wasn't used to. At that moment I was given insight to the true meaning of rebirth. I gazed into the fire realizing that something powerful had transpired here this night. The feelings I was experiencing were powerful and though I didn't really comprehend it all at this moment, the power of the Lord's love.

I wanted so bad to share my experience with Charlie. How did he expect me to sleep, feeling the way I did. But I knew I shouldn't disturb him. I sat there for the longest time staring into the fire. What happened here tonight? I thought to myself. The full understanding of tonight's events was still beyond me. As I sat there rocking, bathed in a warm glowing peace, I couldn't comprehend the new life that was about to greet me.

CHAPTER 8

The next morning I awoke just before dawn. The sun was shedding its first light. As my senses awakened to the new day, I knew something was different. The feelings were still with me from last night. I felt strangely refreshed and new. I sat up in bed when I realized there was no pain. I crawled out of bed, nothing—I couldn't believe it. Over the past several weeks I couldn't move or even breathe without experiencing pain.

"Thank you, Lord, thank you," I said out loud. "Hallelujah! Hallelujah!" I yelled. I hurriedly dressed. I couldn't wait to share my news with Charlie. Red shared my excitement for he was barking and running for the door.

Red darted from room to room, and I was close behind. "Charlie," I yelled. "Good morning Charlie!" Suddenly I noticed the silence that filled the cabin. Charlie was always up humming and whistling. "Where is he?" I thought. God, I wanted to share my feelings with him. Red and I went out onto the porch. I walked around the cabin, but Charlie was nowhere to be found. His pickup sat in the driveway. "Charlie!" I yelled into the morning air, but there was no response.

Suddenly Red ran into the woods. I called after him. He stopped and turned, acting as if he wanted me to follow him. Maybe he smelled the old man's scent. I followed after him. As I chased after my dog, my thoughts were on Charlie. This wasn't like him to leave me. He had been there every morning since he took me in. I began to worry. I had been climbing a slight grade for about fifty yards when Red finally stopped about twenty yards in front of me. He just stood there perfectly still. As I came up beside him, I bent over to catch my breath.

When I looked up, there was the old man. I rubbed my eyes and shook my head. The scene before me seemed surreal. I walked several feet until I was standing at the edge of the clearing. I felt as if I was caught in a dream. About twenty feet away sat Charlie on a small bench made of logs. Ten feet in front of him stood an altar made of stone.

It was maybe twelve to fourteen feet tall with an old wooden cross protruding from the top. The old man's head was bowed in prayer, his forehead resting on his hands. For as long as I live, I will never forget the scene that was before me.

I felt a powerful presence around me. My skin tingled and I couldn't move. Whatever had a hold on me, had a hold on Red too, for he sat perfectly still, not moving a muscle.

The surrounding forest was shedding its coat of darkness, but the clearing where Charlie sat was aglow in light. The sun's rays streaking through the trees bathed the altar in light. I was totally mesmerized by the experience. The old man seemed so at peace when he prayed.

Suddenly I felt as if Red and I were intruders. Surely this was a sacred and private place for the old man. After several minutes, I decided we should leave and wait for Charlie to come back to the cabin. As I turned to go, Charlie motioned for me to come and sit next to him. He never looked to see who was there.

I slowly and quietly walked over and sat down next to him. He opened his eyes and smiled at me. In a soft voice he said, "I didn't know if you'd find me here. Let us pray and give the Lord thanks," he said. I bowed my head and listened to his heartfelt prayer. He gave thanks for all his blessings. He prayed for so may people all over the world that they may come to know God through Jesus Christ. Then he prayed for me. As I sat next to Charlie in prayer, a feeling of serene peace enveloped me to the point it was euphoric. The powerful presence that enveloped this clearing bathed us in warmth and love. I felt a true connection with God sitting next to this gentle old man. Finally he said, "Amen." I did likewise.

We slowly stood up. I was numb from the experience and stumbled to gain my balance. Charlie turned towards me and gave me a big hug. "Bless you, son, bless you, "he whispered. I tried to speak, but no words came out. All I could do was smile at the old man.

The clearing was still aglow with light. "This Ryan, "he said, spreading his arms, "this clearing is my holy of holies. Here I feel closer to God than anywhere else in the world."

We turned and headed back to the cabin. "Ryan, when I first came out here, a vision came to me one night and showed that clearing to me. I was instructed to build an altar to God and so I did. Ryan I am so blessed to feel His mercy and witness His awesome glory. His presence and love are all we need for this journey throughout life."

I longed to share Charlie's deep faith in God. When he spoke of his love for God, he was always so contented, so at peace.

After breakfast, we read a few passages from the Bible and gave another prayer of thanks. Whatever he asked me to do, I now did without question or hesitation. My trust had been firmly entrusted to him.

"Ryan, I'm sure you feel quite different this morning," he said softly.

"Yes, Charlie," I said in excitement, remembering how my pain was gone. "Charlie may pain in my chest and my head, I woke up this morning and all the pain is gone."

"Oh, hallelujah, hallelujah!" he bellowed. "Thank you, Lord, thank you." Then looking at me seriously, he continued. "Son, the glorious feeling you are experiencing, open yourself up to it. Allow it to grow and flourish inside of you for it is God's love flowing in you. Surrender yourself to its power and beauty for you are in the palms of our loving God. Know and trust that he lives within you, within each one of us.

I sat mesmerized and honored for the gift of wisdom the old man was bestowing upon me. "Your new life, son, your renewed relationship to God will transform your life if you will allow it. And for your relationship with God to flourish, it must be nurtured in fertile ground. You must daily communicate with Him through your thought and your prayers. Place your trust and your faith in the knowledge that God loves you. And as a parent only wishes good things for their children, imagine the wonderful things God wants for you."

The meaning of Charlie's words touched my heart. As my eyes met his, the old man continued, "Ryan, you can walk through life never to worry again if only you will carry this belief in faith: *If God be for us, who would be against us*. Turn all your worries and your problems over to Him, for he will lift their burden from your shoulders for all eternity." Charlie looked at me and smiled. "I haven't worried for over forty years, Ryan. Why should I when He gladly does it for you."

I shook my head. I had never thought of God in this way before. He is truly on our side, if we will let Him. And then it came to me, the full meaning of Charlie's statement. If God be for us, who would be against us. If I would place my heart and soul in faith with God, who or what could ever harm me, really, with God by my side?

The old man stood up from the table and his bellowing voice, "Oh, Ryan, it is a glorious day, a glorious day indeed! We have so much to be thankful for, but we also have much work to do before you leave here."

His words struck me hard. I had become so entranced in my experience here that I had lost all thought of time or of leaving and I had no idea of all this work he kept talking about. My month was nearly up, but I knew I couldn't leave until our work was finished, no matter what the cost. I would ask Charlie to drive me to town tomorrow morning so I could extend my stay. I wondered how everyone would react to my desire to stay longer.

CHAPTER 9

The next morning after breakfast, Charlie, Red and I climbed into his old truck and headed for the town of Pines. Charlie said it was about a forty minute drive. Pines was a small town of about six hundred people. It consisted of a general store, a lumber mill, a tavern/restaurant and some shops and a garage. This was where Charlie came to stock up.

As we drove through the forest, my mind began to wander. I hadn't been in touch with anyone back home since I left. How would they react to my staying even longer? Would they understand my need to stay?

Finally, we came to the main road that would lead us to Pines. Charlie turned onto the road and after shifting through the old truck's gears he looked over and smiled. "You seem rather quiet this morning, Ryan, a little nervous calling home?" I shook my head yes. The old man must have sensed my lack of desire to converse, and he looked straight ahead, humming as we headed down the road.

I was anxious about calling home. There was definitely a change taking place in me, and how would I ever explain what was happening to me when I didn't totally understand myself. How would I explain the spiritual and mystical energy of Charlie's Woods? They would all think that I had lost my mind in Montana. Still, I had no choice. I couldn't leave, not now.

We passed the lumber mill just outside of Pines. As we drove down Main Street, the townspeople were busy going about their business. It felt strange to be out among people again.

Everyone knew Charlie. They either called out his name or waved. Red was excited by the activity, too, his tail wagging back and forth. Charlie pointed out the different stores and businesses, telling me a little history about them.

He pulled into a parking space in front of the general store. A phone booth was located at the end of the building next to a vacant lot. I climbed out of the truck with Red right behind me. Charlie climbed out and told me to come into the store. "I want to introduce you to Big Jim," he said. As we walked through the open door it was as if I had stepped back in time. The store was dark, but clean. It had old hardwood floors and shelves. The merchandise was neatly displayed on the shelves. After my introduction to Big Jim, and believe me, the name fit, Charlie said he had a few people to see. "I'll be back in about twenty minuets or so. Big Jim is going to let you use his phone. I thought it would be more private than you using the public telephone out front." I thanked him, and he turned and walked out of the store.

Big Jim came around the counter and placed his hand on my shoulder. "Ryan," he said, in a deep baritone voice, "any friend of Charlie's is a friend of mine. Come, I'll show you where the phone is." He led me through the back of the store into a small office. He pointed to the phone and his chair. "Make yourself at home," he said, "and just come out when you finish." I thanked him as he turned to go wait on a customer.

I sat for several minutes wondering who to call first, and what I would say. Finally I took a deep breath and dialed my boss's number. I might as well get this out of the way first. My boss informed me that if I wasn't back by the beginning of the week, he couldn't promise me I would still have my job. "You know I had to pull strings to get you an entire month off," he said.

"I know, I answered, "but something has come up and I can't leave yet."

"Do you have any idea when you'll be back?" he asked.

"I don't know. It could be several more weeks. I can't give you a definite date," I said.

"The owner isn't going to be very receptive to this, and to be perfectly honest, Ryan, I don't understand it either. I'll take it to the owner, but I doubt he's going to approve it. We need your territory covered. I'll do what I can." He didn't sound very reassuring. He wished me good luck and I thanked him. I hung up the phone. I couldn't believe it. My first contact with reality back home and it was a crisis. Man, I couldn't lose my job, but I couldn't leave here yet. I knew something good was happening to me here, something that would impact the rest of my life. For a moment I felt the fear and anxiety of losing my job. I couldn't imagine the ridicule I would receive if I lost my position because of this trip. People would think I had gone mad. I could see my ex-wife pouncing on the opportunity to show that I was an unfit and irresponsible father. Reality was back with a vengeance. But then a remarkable thing happened. That voice, I heard it again: "I am with you always, I am the light out of the darkness." I quickly looked around Big Jim's small office. I was all alone. A quiet calm came over me and pushed the anxiety and fear I was feeling away. Suddenly, I didn't care what any of these people thought. Something kept telling me what they thought wasn't important.

For the first time in my life I was ready to risk my job. My coming out here and my decision to stay longer were giant steps for me. Though I didn't see it at the time, these were Giant steps of faith.

My next call was to Steve. I talked to him briefly and he assured me everything was fine. He told me to stay as long as necessary, that between him and Sarah they would take care of my house. I asked him how Sarah was doing, and he informed me she was fine, but worried sick about me. "She really loves you, Ryan," he said. "I hope you're going to call her."

"I am," I replied, "after I call my son." Steve pressed me for details about my trip. I told him I would explain everything when I got home, but that he might not recognize the person who was his best friend. Again, he wished me luck.

"Dad, is that you?" the boyish little voice said through the phone. I couldn't hold back my tears of joy hearing his little voice. The impact of how much I missed him hit hard. "When are you coming home?" he asked. I told him how much I loved him and how much I missed him. I searched for the words to explain that I wouldn't be coming home for a while yet.

"Brent, Daddy needs to take care of some business before I come home," I said. "But I promise I'll bee home as soon as I can, probably in a couple of weeks." The disappointment in his voice broke my heart. Again, I told him how much I loved him and to put his mom on the phone so I could tell her my plans. She said it was fine with her and there was no problem keeping Brent. But I could also hear the antagonism in her voice. I was sure she wondered what I was up to.

I took several deep breaths before I dialed Sarah's number. I realized now why I saved her for last. Calling her stirred the most fear and anxiety, though I was calm in my decision to stay. I wondered how she would react to my call. Was Steve right that she still loves me or was I testing her patience to the breaking point? And how would she feel about me staying longer at the risk of losing my job? Would she, too think I had gone crazy? As I heard her phone ring, my stomach was in knots. "Hello," came her soft angelic voice. At first I couldn't speak. "Hello," she said again.

"Sarah," I said hesitantly.

"Ryan, Ryan, is that really you?" The excitement in her voice was unmistakable.

"Yes, it's really me," I answered.

"How are you? Are you okay? I have been worried about you."

"I'm fine Sarah, really I'm fine."

"Ryan, somebody named Charlie called and said you had been beaten, oh I have been so worried about you."

"I'm fine, Sarah, really I'm okay."

"Oh, Ryan, I've missed you so much." And then I heard her voice break down and start to cry. Suddenly I felt awful for not calling her sooner. I realized what I must be putting her through, all this time without a word.

"I'm sorry, Ryan. I didn't mean to cry, but I'm so happy to hear your voice. I love you. Ryan. I love you so much." Her voice was filled with emotion.

"Sarah, I love you, too, and I'm so sorry to put you through all of this." She started to cry again. "Sarah, don't cry, please don't cry," I pleaded.

"I'm just so happy and relieved," she said, regaining her composure. "Did you find your answers, Ryan? Where are you anyway? Oh, your voice is music to my ears," she replied. "When are you coming home?" she asked.

"Slow down," I said. "I can only answer one question at a time," I joked. Then I heard her laugh on the other end. "Thank you, Lord," I said.

"Oh, how I want to feel your arms around me, Ryan, how soon will you be home?" she added, impatiently.

"Sarah, that's part of the reason I'm calling. I need to stay awhile longer."

"How much longer?" she asked.

"Several weeks. But I'm not exactly sure on the time. And, Sarah, I might have lost my job, too." She was silent.

"Ryan, what's going on, this sounds too mysterious. Are you sure about this?"

"Yes, Sarah, I am sure. I can't explain everything on the phone and you might not believe me anyway." I assured her that I knew without a doubt that I was where I was supposed to be and that the answers I was seeking I would find here. I just hoped she'd recognize me when I arrived home. I told her a little about Charlie, which triggered a thousand more questions.

I promised her that I would call her as soon as I was ready to come back. "Sarah, I know this probably doesn't make a lot of sense, but trust me on this. Your love and understanding mean more to me than you know. Sarah, something good, something amazing is happening here and that's why I can't leave yet. I must see this through. It means so much that you're still there for me."

"Ryan," she said softly, "I will always be here for you. Never forget that." Her words stuck in my heart. We said our goodbyes. I sat for the longest time just holding the telephone receiver in my hand. Slowly I sat the receiver sown. I had a sudden urge to pray.

I bowed my head and asked the Lord to forgive me for my past whining and complaining. These phone calls made me realize how blessed I was. I knew in my heart that I had more riches than any king and that I had blinded myself to the true blessings God had given me.

Slowly I got up and walked to the front of the store. I thanked Big Jim for the use of his phone and asked him to let me know how much I owed him. He smiled, shook my hand and said, "Charlie had already taken care of it." Why didn't that surprise me?

I looked out the store window and there sat the old man in his truck. He smiled and waved. Red jumped in the back of the truck and I climbed in the front. Charlie turned the key and the motor roared to life. "Everything okay back home?" he asked before pulling away.

"Everything's fine, Charlie, at least I think it is." I replied. "They probably all think I'm a bit crazy," I said with a chuckle.

"Nothing to be concerned about," he said smiling. "I've had a few people think that of me."

We both laughed as we headed home.

As we drove down the highway, I shared with Charlie my phone conversations. I shared with him how blessed I felt to have such a wonderful women as Sarah. "She loves you very much, Ryan, I can tell," he said. "And what a wonderful son you have."

"I know Charlie, and it broke my heart to tell him I wasn't coming home. I miss him so!"

And I shared how thankful I was to Sarah and Steve for taking care of my home and garden while I was here. He looked at me smiling. "What?" I asked.

"Do you feel its power?" he asked.

"What power?" I replied.

"The power of being thankful. Think how good you feel right now, that is the wonder, the gift of being thankful for your blessings. Now do you see why I give thanks everyday?" I shook my head and smiled back. Oh, he certainly is a wise man. I thought. It did feel good to feel thankful.

"And what about your work?" Charlie asked. "Were they understanding?"

I shook my head. "I don't know, Charlie," I said. "I don't have a good feeling about that. I most likely will lose my job over this."

He turned off the main road and we started through the forest. He pulled over and stopped the truck. He looked at me with sincerity. "And how do you feel about that son?" he asked. "Well at first I was filled with anxiety and fear," I replied, "but then a sense of calm came over me and I heard the voice I heard the other night." The old man smiled at me. "Charlie, I can't leave until it's finished," I blurted out.

"Good, good," he said. "You're learning to listen." He placed his giant hand on mine. "Son, God doesn't give bad advice. Remember today, because you passed a big test of faith. Remember God is on your side, He will take care of you." A big grin spread across his face as he put the truck in gear and stepped on the gas.

As we turned on the road that led to Charlie's home, the storm that we had been driving on the edge of finally let loose. Claps of thunder and streaks of lightening filled the sky. Slowly drops of rain hit the windshield, and then grew with greater intensity.

I watched Charlie driving as the storm pounced upon us. "Beautiful, just beautiful," he commented. He whistled, hummed as we bounced down the road. Love and peace and gratitude for life emanated from this kind and wonderful old man. I could feel it whenever I was in his presence. I leaned back against the seat and closed my eyes. My thoughts turned to my phone conversations. Charlie said I had passed a test of faith, but had I? Now a small part of me was questioning my decision to stay at the risk of my job. I never would have made such a risky decision before. Something about me had changed, there was no doubting that. The embers of doubt inside me were trying to flare up again. I wondered if part of what I would find here was the deep unshakable faith that Charlie had found. I hope so.

CHAPTER 10

After a casual lunch we went out and sat on the porch. The sky was clear, the storm had gone. "Charlie," I said, "Do you mind if I ask you something?"

"Ask away," he joyfully responded.

"Well," I started, "When I came out here I was surely a lost and ungrateful soul. Today when I made these phone calls I realized how blessed I am. Why, then, am I still so confused? And what about my risking my job, isn't that being irresponsible? And everything that is happening to me, I don't know what this all means."

"Whoa, whoa, Ryan, one question at a time," he responded. "Now, first of all, you are starting to worry again. Worry serves no positive purpose, that's why God tells us to turn all our worries over to Him. And, son, that takes faith. Old habits are hard to break and that's part of what you are experiencing. Faith, like trust, needs to be worked at, it won't come overnight.

"Faith is an all or nothing deal," he continued. "Either you have it or you don't. You can't say "I have a little faith, because that is a contradiction. Complete faith means having no doubts. Total faith is the only way to have a deep personal relationship with God.

"It's one of the major problems in our world today. Too many people worry too much. They worry about things that more often than not never become a reality. They allow their worries to slowly suffocate the life right out of them until their lives are filled with only worry. Their constant worries turn into fear, and bitterness, that attracts a host of other negative forces, like jealousy, low self esteem, and blame. Soon they convince themselves that all the misfortune of their lives is someone else's fault, totally shirking any responsibility for their own despair, for their own choices.

"Why do you think Jesus tells us in the Bible that worry is a sin? He does so because it produces nothing positive, only negative. It's not even real Ryan. This is part of the work we need to do. To practice the act of faith daily, to break the old habits and realize the power of absolute faith in our loving God will remove worry from our life forever."

His words were powerful and I hungered for more. "Ryan," he continued, "everything you are feeling and thinking is normal. You have just started to experience a new revelation of God's love through Christ. The feeling is euphoric and beautiful. You feel peace and love as you have never felt before. You want to hold it tightly and never let it go."

"But then, all the events and feelings and experiences, all that makes you who you are today, tries to come back and pull you down. Your human nature wants to return to its comfort zone, no matter how much misery and despair comes along with it."

"But, why, Charlie? I mean, to hear you say that, well it doesn't make any sense," I stated.

"No, it doesn't," the old man replied. "But you see, in God's infinite wisdom, he knew that for us to truly experience the purity of His love we must, by our own choice, choose to go to Him. God knew that the true wonder of His creation would never be realized if we were forced to love Him. Oh, Ryan, the heartache He must feel by the many choices we make! But His precious gift of free will, which He gives to all of us, He also reveals His true unselfish and unconditional love. This is a perfect love which is impossible for us to experience with another human being."

"Think abut it Ryan, all your life you have witnessed, at least from your own perception, conditional love."

"That's not true," I protested.

"I never said it was necessarily true, only our perception. As a child do you feel your parents love you more when you're good or bad? As a child, growing up we relate to this ideal. It's our motivation to be good and to please our parents. When do they shower us with love and praise? When we're good, right? Now don't get me wrong, Ryan, our parents love us, we love our children and our spouses. But the way we have learned to express our love is usually conditionally."

"Now what comes along with this personal perception of conditional love is that when we displease and anger, when we hurt the ones we love, we begin to form the perception that we do not deserve, or we're unworthy of their love. Now, granted, this is only a perception because real love is unconditional. But when we start to feel unworthy, unloved, then the seeds of evil have found a place to grow."

His words gave me new insight to my own feelings and experiences. He stood up and walked to the edge of the porch. Suddenly he turned towards me, looking at me thoughtfully. The next words out of his mouth bowled me over, for he answered my questions before I could ask it. "This is why, son, you feel unworthy of Sarah's love. This is why you are creating such a struggle and a crisis in your life, by not allowing yourself to commit your love to her."

I shook my head. "I don't know how you know what you know, Charlie," I said. "But you are right. I've been grappling with that question since I talked to her today." I walked over to the edge of the porch next to the old man, staring out through the trees. "What do I do about it, Charlie?" I asked. "I certainly don't want to hurt her."

"I know you don't," he replied. "Open your heart and allow her love to flow in unconditionally. Erase any false perceptions you may have because they are not hers. She loves you for who you are, your good qualities and your faults. Allow her love to help strengthen and inspire you, to complete you."

I know a true love like Sarah's is new to you. And when we

experience something powerful and new in our lives we rush to find an explanation for it, to define it if you will."

"Come, let's go inside. I want to show you something." We walked inside and he motioned for me to sit at the table. "Ryan," he said, gesturing with his arms, pointing to the rows and rows of books filling the room, "here in all the millions and millions of beautiful words written by these wonderful authors are the lessons of life and secrets of happiness. God gave us the wonders of communicating with each other. No other creature has the creative freedom or ability to communicate as we do. In all these thousands and thousands of books are creative and passionate writers who wish to reach out to their fellow man and share the magnificent adventure we call life. Some wish to share life's good fortunes, others valuable life lessons learned out of heartache and despair. Others wish to inspire us to reach the stars. Still others try to explain the meaning of life and our purpose in it. Oh, my Ryan, so much can be learned by picking up a good book and reading it! The reading of a few books helped change my life and I've been reading steadily ever since. This is why I call this my library of life."

I sat there wondering how anyone could ever read so many books. "Yes, I've read nearly every book here, Ryan," the old man commented. I still swear he could read my thoughts. "But one book in particular means more to me than all the others." He walked over and uncovered his Bible. He clutched it to his chest and held it close as a mother would a child.

"Forty two years ago a dear lady gave me this precious book, shortly after I almost took my life."

Charlie noticed my look of surprise.

"I know Betsy shared my story with you, it's why you have so many questions about me." I smiled and shook my head. He smiled and continued. "I was sitting in Central Park alone, trying to understand the meaning of the visions I had witnessed. I had a new thirst for life because I knew my wife and daughter were at peace in heaven, but still, the voice saying I had a work to do mystified me."

"Then a kind lady sat down next to me on the park bench. We exchanged hellos and chatted for a brief time. She told me she sensed my turmoil and my need of help to find my way out of the darkness. I sat back, stunned by her forwardness, but amazed at her accuracy. She reached into her bag and pulled out this book," Charlie said, pointing at the Bible.

"She handed me this Bible, and as I took it from her she touched my hand. I can still remember the incredible warmth and feeling of comfort that ran through me. I told her I already owned several Bibles. She just smiled. "Please," she said, "I want you to have this one." I thanked her. She got up to leave and made this last comment: "Open your heart to Jesus, receive his love and forgiveness, and share it with all you meet. Walk in faith." She smiled and walked away. I sat there holding her Bible when I noticed how beautiful and unique her gift was. I had never seen a Bible like this. I couldn't take such an exquisite gift from a stranger, so I jumped up and ran after her. She was nowhere in sight. It was like she had vanished. I tucked the book inside my coat and waked home. I gave it no more thought until retiring for the night."

"There on the table sat the Bible she gave me. I found myself continuously looking at it as if guided by some unseen force. Finally I went over and picked it up. I notice how soft the leather cover felt in my hands, and the more I looked at it the more I appreciated what a fine book this was. The cover had been handcrafted; the leather work truly was exquisite. The pages edges sparkled in the light as if they were trimmed in gold. I slowly opened the cover and found these words written inside."

"Dear Charlie," he looked up at me, his eyes wide as he relived the memory. "Ryan," he said, "I never told her my name."

"Dear Charlie, in these pages are the secrets to a joyous and fulfilling life. To uncover the secrets, these pages must be studied, not just read. Each day, morning and evening, study a few chapters and soon the secrets will reveal themselves to you. But first, study the passages I have outlined here for you. They will open the door to a new and wonderful life. Surrender yourself to their meaning and ask Christ to come into your heart. You will experience a glorious rebirth. Always remember we are all joyous blessings of God and His love is the eternal flame of hope that burns in our hearts. Know He is always with you, in good times and in bad, and take absolute comfort in that knowledge. You have been chosen to share His message of love and hope with those in need. The Lord will guide you on your journey. Take time to be still and pray to Him. In time another will be sent to you, lost in his own confusion, struggling to escape the darkness of his own making. He will be chosen too, for he has been blessed with a gift that his own turmoil has blinded him from seeing. You will help him see and you will pass this treasured text onto him, a new generation to carry God's message to the world. Take joy in living and experience your days in thankfulness."

His eyes were wet with tears as he closed the book. He looked at me. "There was no signature," he said. "But the profound impact she had on my life lives on this day.

"You see Ryan, forty two years ago I completely surrendered myself to the Lord and accepted Jesus Christ onto my heart, just as you did the other evening. You see, she had marked the same passages that I had you read, so when I promise a new life in God, I'm talking from experience."

"God led me to this wilderness where I settled. Money no longer carried the importance in my life it once had. After buying this property, I donated much of my money to missionaries and charities, keeping enough to help those in need, like you, and to take care of my basic needs. I have never felt happier or more fulfilled in my life."

I sat, awestruck by his story, his honesty and his openness. He walked over to where he kept his sacred Bible and wrapped it back in its cover. He returned and sat down across from me.

"Charlie," I said, "but why am I really here? Why would I be chosen to come out here and meet you? I'm nobody, Charlie, to be chosen. I'm not really worthy of all this." He looked at me and smiled.

"Oh, but you are. Son, God so loved the whole world, and he must have something very special in mind for you."

I just stared at the old man. I was totally dumbfounded and confused by his last statement. This was all too bizarre for me to comprehend. Charlie must have noticed my confused look. "Son, be patient, your answers will come soon, just be patient."

We got up and walked outside. The storm was long gone. There was freshness in the air. "Glorious, isn't it, Ryan?" Charlie said, "Just glorious," as he took a deep breath, breathing in the clean fresh air.

Charlie had some chores to do. I offered to help, but he told me to take the time to think over what we had just discussed. "Clear your mind, Ryan, and just listen to your thoughts, really listen to them for in them you will recognize God's voice. Learn to be still."

I decided to take a little walk, but I couldn't empty my mind. So much had transpired this day with all the emotions of calling back home. I tried not worrying about my job, but how could I not? And this wise old man telling me I was chosen to be here, there was no way I could clear my mind of all these thoughts.

Later that night I tossed and turned in my bed. All kinds of thoughts filled my mind. What was going to happen here and what lay ahead of me? I wondered if forty two years ago Charlie struggled with the knowledge of being mysteriously chosen as I was now. I would barely sleep at all tonight.

CHAPTER 11

The next morning we started in earnest the work Charlie talked about. On the table were two sets of books: the Bible, *Evening By Evening* by Charles Spurgeon and yes that small maroon paper back, *My Utmost For His Highest* by Oswald Chambers. I couldn't believe my eyes.

I shared with Charlie how the other day I was drawn to that book, and didn't understand why. Now it was there on the table.

The old man shook his head and chuckled. "Oh, Ryan, you have so much to learn. Ye of little faith," he said. "God is guiding us all the time. This is why faith is paramount in having a real relationship with God. To believe in the unseen, which many times is God's loving and guiding hands pointing the way." I sat there trying to fully comprehend his words when he continued. "You see Ryan, many times your walk in faith will defy your natural common sense. But as you learn to trust your faith and abandon your sense of logic, faith will become a powerful and guiding force in your daily life.

"Walking in faith does take some getting used to, especially for a rookie," he said with a laugh. "But remember, Ryan, that God is always watching over you as he does all of us. And take comfort in this truth.

"I think I get it Charlie, I think I really understand what you're saying."

"Good, good," he said. "There is hope for you." Smiling he motioned for me to sit at the table.

Then he asked me to open *My Utmost for His Highest* to

today's date and to read aloud today's message. We took turns reading to each other then we opened the Bible starting with the New Testament and read several chapters from the book of John. Afterwards we prayed.

We repeated this ritual every morning and evening. Charlie reminded me to always make part of my prayers a prayer of thanks. Each day my new spirit grew and blossomed under Charlie's watchful and caring eye. A new vibrant inner strength was replacing my old fears and insecurities. Peace love and compassion were now a living part of me because of God's love for me and this kind old man.

I now understood why we read the Bible and daily devotional together. The devotional helped to connect my personal life with truths from the scriptures. There were many days when these passages seemed to be speaking directly to me, and for the first time in my life reading the Bible carried clarity and new understanding, not just the reading of some words.

My new life was very different from the old one and my faith in the unseen was tested daily. Jesus said that having faith was as natural as breathing. I was slowly coming to the realization of that truth.

Over the next several weeks I was both honored and blessed with Charlie's teachings. Our days were filled with long talks on a wide range of topics. We discussed religion, philosophy, self improvement and spiritual growth. He shared his vast knowledge of biographies of great men in history and their mortal impact on mankind. We read everyday from his library of life. I was in awe of the depth of his knowledge on all these topics.

We took long walks through these majestic woods embracing the incredible beauty of God's creation. On these walks I would be amazed at the incredible joy the old man got from the simple pleasures of life. He would be like a child seeing a butterfly or a beautiful flower for the first time. His living example set in me an appreciation for life that I hadn't felt before.

Twice daily, morning and evening, time was set aside for

our spiritual relationship with God. Charlie derived so much pleasure form this as did I.

Each morning after breakfast we would visit this altar and pray. Then back at the cabin we would study passages from the Bible and read from our daily devotional by Oswald Chambers, *My Utmost for His Highest*.

I cherished the time we spent together. We prayed daily. Charlie said praying was just talking to God, simple heartfelt talks. "Can't have a relationship with God if you won't talk to Him," he'd say.

One afternoon as we were on one of our daily walks, Charlie said he wanted to share a special place with me. We had been walking half an hour or so when I noticed a clearing up ahead. I so enjoyed our walks together. Charlie was constantly teaching and sharing experiences of life. As we got closer to the clearing, Charlie slowed his pace. Finally, he turned to me. "Out there," he said, pointing to the clearing "is one of God's masterpieces. I'm so filled with joy that I can share this with you, Ryan. This is one of my favorite places to visit on all the earth." The old man truly had my curiosity going, because from here I couldn't understand the exuberance. He smiled and continued on. When we reached the clearing, the afternoon sun bathed our faces with warmth. We stopped to catch our breath. I was mystified by Charlie's stamina, for he was nearly twice my age. And there were times when I could barely keep up with him. We walked a little further to the top of the knoll. A spectacular field of wild flowers unfolded before us. The meadow was filled with a spectacular array of wild flowers, gently swaying in the breeze. Off in the distance, a heard of deer grazed, stopping their eating momentarily to check us out. Charlie pointed to the sky where a pair of bald eagles soared high above us. Butterflies danced from flower to flower and the sounds of birds singing filled the air. Off in the distance, you could see snow covered mountain peaks. The old man turned to me, a giant grin on his face. "Isn't this just glorious, Ryan?" he said, excitement filling his voice.

"Yes," I replied, "It's beautiful."

Then he continued walking ahead of me. After about fifty yards, he stopped. I was so mesmerized by the beauty that surrounded me; I hadn't seen him walk off. He yelled for me to join him. As I walked towards him I realized I heard rushing water. I wondered where it was coming from. As I got closer to him, I finally saw. He was standing on the edge of a gorge. There was a spectacular waterfall on the other side that dropped into the gorge at least several hundred feet to the bottom. Everything seemed so fresh, so clean around us. The sheer grandeur of this place was stunning. The kaleidoscope of sight and sound filled my senses with feelings of euphoria. Charlie smiled and I smiled back.

"This is quite a masterpiece, Charlie," I finally said. His eyes sparkled with delight.

"Oh Ryan," he said, "Every time I come here it's always like the first time. Everything is so alive, nature beating in harmonious perfection. Can you feel the peace and tranquility that surrounds us?" he asked.

"Yes, I do, Charlie. Yes I do."

Raising his arms to the sky, he shouted in his bellowing voice, "Oh, thank you, Lord. Thank you for this beautiful place!"

He looked at me more serious. "Ryan, I pray that the state of Montana honors my wishes and never allows anyone to compromise the beauty that surrounds us here. Come, let us sit and rest a spell."

"Okay," I said.

"Ryan, he said in his gentle voice, "Whenever I slip a little, or start to take for granted the precious gift of life, I come here to regain my perspective on the beauty of life. People are in such a rush these days. They remind of ants scurrying about their duties, never taking the time to appreciate the beauty of life. They excuse their bodies and their minds, but totally neglect their spiritual connection to God. They scurry about at a dizzying pace so they can posses more material wealth, but the more they posses, the more they want. Happiness and contentment are always just another possession. Suddenly they are old and their constant pursuit of more has left them tired and empty.

"The sad part is that they always had choices. Oh, what a dangerous gift God gave us, choice." He squeezed his thumb and forefinger together and then parted them slightly. "If they would have only taken a tiny bit of time each day to be still and allow their inner voice to speak, to nurture their spirit, to hear God's voice, they would have experienced a life greater than they have ever known. But people convince themselves they can't afford to take time for themselves; others are afraid of facing their inner voice, for they know the life they are living is out of control and morally empty. In their arrogance and ignorance they try to convince themselves that they can only get themselves out of the mess they have made out of their lives. Oh, Ryan, if they would just take the time to be still and be with God—oh, what a pity."

I nodded my head in agreement, I marveled at the simplicity of his wisdom.

"Ryan, often I come here to meditate, and give thanks to God and become one with the beauty around me. Now close your eyes and take a slow deep breath. Slowly clear your mind of all thoughts until there is only one voice, one source of thought. Allow yourself total peace. Breathe in the beauty that is all around you; lose yourself of its majesty. When your mind is clear, be still and listen. His voice will be your highest thoughts. Give it total freedom for in your stillness will come the answers you seek."

Part of the old man's teachings was learning to meditate. At first it seemed tortuous to sit still for more than a few minutes, but each time we meditated the more natural it became. Meditation, like my daily prayer time, became a spiritual connection to God.

As I sat with my eyes closed in this majestic setting, I could feel the harmonious song of nature, a connection with the universe. As my mind cleared, I became one with everything around me. As my own vibrations mixed harmoniously with the universe around me, I felt the importance of each one of us harmonizing with the universe. And though we are only a single note in a great cosmic song, all of us add to the song's clarity and beauty. Suddenly, I was filled with the understanding of how connected all of us really are and if we would just listen to His commandment to love one another, each one of us could help the world. The voice I heard was so real. "Love one another as I have loved you." I didn't want to leave this place. I felt so loved, so at peace.

Charlie slowly rose to his feet, distracting me out of my meditative state. It took several minutes to regain my senses. Charlie put his arm around me as we started our hike home.

I shared with Charlie my experience and what the voice said to me.

"So," he said in a commanding voice, "there is hope, yes there is real hope for the world, but God needs many messengers to touch people's hearts and souls. You're to be one of His messengers, Ryan."

I stopped walking and stared at him. He looked at me and laughed. "What's the matter, Ryan?" he asked quizzically.

I stuttered," Wh-what did you just say?"

He laughed again at my reaction. "You're to be a messenger of hope and inspiration."

"How? Why? How?" I asked. "How can I inspire anyone else?" I was confused.

He touched my shoulder. "Ryan, the answer will come to you before you leave here. Be patient and listen. Have faith."

The rest of the walk back, well, I was in a trance, confused about what lay ahead of me. One truth was becoming very clear. God's plan is not always our plan. Though it still wasn't clear how, I knew that I would leave this place a very different man.

CHAPTER 12

The next morning after breakfast I sat rocking on the porch. I still could not believe all that happened to me since my arrival. Day by day, week by week, a new and very different me was emerging. The only way for me to even try to explain the change in me was, well, I was changing from the inside out. From deep in my soul, my new spirit was emerging. I was beginning to understand, to really comprehend the message, "Ye must be born again." These words precisely described what was happening to me. Slowly, like a new baby emerging from his mother's womb, the new me was being given new life.

At first I wasn't aware of the change taking place in me, but day by day my new life was being nurtured and refreshed by our loving God.

Nearly two months had passed and my whole perspective of life had been drastically altered. Our daily praying, our daily giving of thanks, our daily readings, all were molding me into a new man. Yes, it really was a rebirth.

As I sat there rocking, reflecting on my time here, I felt so blessed. Never had I felt so at peace with who I was, or so loved as I did now. My feelings of insecurity, of failure, had all disappeared. As my thoughts turned to all the people in my life, they all took on a new appearance. I felt only thankfulness for all those I was close to. I felt a new depth of love and compassion. I now knew that Sarah being in my life was orchestrated by God, and instead of fearing her love, I now eagerly embraced it. The love for my son, I never thought it possible to love him more than I did, but even that, God made dearer to me. I had new insights and a new purpose of being a father.

To those in my life I didn't feel close to or even like, I now cast no judgment.

I suddenly realized that all my negative and destructive thoughts had vanished; they were gone, just gone, buried. I stood up, straight and tall, filling my lungs with the clear crisp air, thrusting my chest out, then slowly exhaling. The very revelation of the new man living inside me was overwhelming. The sheer joy I was feeling, I can't find the words to describe!

How, you ask, can such a transformation be possible? Only one way, by the grace and love of God flowing through as living water through this special, kind old man named Charlie. The sheer power of love, true unconditional love I could envision, as I stood there lost in my thoughts, the very transformation of mankind if we would honor Christ's last commandment; "Love one another, as I have loved you." The impact of the understanding of this simple truth jolted me, for now I clearly understood our connection to one another. Our feeling of insignificance is demolished by this truth. For we are all responsible for each other, our actions; our feelings are truly significant to each other. I felt as if God were giving me a small glimpse of His glory.

The old man appeared on the porch. I buried my head in my hands. "Thank you, Lord, thank you," I said. I looked up, shaking my head, Charlie smiled at me. "Charlie," I said, my voice somewhat quivering, "Would you please sit down?" He walked over and sat down next to me. I slowly shared my experience and my thoughts. He listened intently, nodding his head. When I finished, he sat quietly for a moment, studying me. Then he closed his eyes and I heard him softly say, "Thank you, Lord. Thank you, sweet Jesus." He looked at me and smiled.

"Oh, Ryan, how His spirit has grown in you these past months. What a blessing it is for me to witness the spirit of God in you. God bless you son, God bless you."

I felt very special in Charlie's presence. How could I ever thank him for saving my life? For he had in two short months, become a significant part of my life. He had become my mentor. I so cared for and admired the old man. His gift of love and caring was beyond measure. I watched him as he rocked in his chair, that look of serene peace that was truly a part of him.

All his joy came from serving God. His deep faith opened God's kingdom to him. His commitment to helping his fellow man was true and pure.

"Charlie," I said in a low voice. He looked over to me.

"Yes, Ryan, what is it?" he asked.

"Charlie, I just want you to know that I love you and am eternally grateful for you in my life." My voice filled with emotion.

He smiled and replied, "I love you too, son."

We stood up and hugged each other.

After lunch we walked to Charlie's special place. On our way he said this was a very special day. And we would have a celebration dinner this evening.

"What are we celebrating?" I asked.

He looked at me and smiled. "I'll tell you this evening," he replied. As we reached the clearing, the magnificent beauty of this place always took my breath away. A powerful divine presence filled Charlie's Woods, but especially so at his alter and here. You were filled with a deep feeling of belonging, of peace and love. This powerful presence which once was mysterious and somewhat frightening, was no longer so. I was filled with the spirit of Christ, was a new man with new eyes to see.

We sat down at our usual spot and reveled in the beauty that surrounded us. Charlie gave a prayer of thanks and then we meditated for over an hour.

While in meditation, my visions returned of me speaking before large groups of people, sharing the gift of our salvation in Christ and God's glory in us learning how to love one another. I was totally consumed by the experience. When I finished my meditation, I shared the experience with Charlie. "What does all this mean?" I asked. He looked at me and smiled.

"Oh, ye of little faith," he said. "Did I not tell you that you are special, that you have been blessed with a gift?" he said.

"But what gift, Charlie? I still don't understand."

"You will," he replied, "be patient."

We spent the rest of the afternoon walking along the gorge and sharing our thoughts and feelings with one another. Charlie shared some of his memories of others who had passed through here.

That evening Charlie put together a very special dinner, fresh brook trout that he himself had caught earlier that morning, fresh potatoes and onions, corn from Betsy's garden. We cooked outside over an open fire. The heavenly aroma of our meal soon filled the air. It reminded me of my camping trips with Sara. I so missed her and couldn't wait to wrap my arms around her again.

"You'll have good news for her soon," Charlie said, that look of knowing in his eyes. He loved teasing me like this.

"And who will I have good news for?" I asked.

"Why that beautiful lady of yours," he said. 'How, how oh never mind," I said, shaking my head. He never admitted he knew my thoughts but what other explanation was there? "What news will I have to tell her?" I asked. He had my curiosity going.

"Oh, we'll talk after dinner," he said, with a chuckle. I resigned myself that he would tell me when he was ready.

We ate slowly, savoring each and every bite. I don't ever remember enjoying a meal more than I did this one. Everything was delicious.

"Oh, Charlie," I said, rising back in my chair, "I can't eat another bite."

The old man smiled. "I'm glad you enjoyed it," he said.

The evening sun cast a parade of shadows among the trees. The sounds of life sprung up around us as various animals and birds busied themselves to feed. Charlie poured us each a cup of tea. We sat back, observing the beauty that surrounded us. I was convinced that God put a glimpse of heaven on earth to stir our imaginations to the sheer glory of His creation. The old man and I smiled at one another as we drank our tea.

After a while Charlie sat his cup down. "Ryan," he said with a sincere and purposeful voice, "you have grown in so many ways since we first met. You've been a wonderful student, and a treasured friend. Someday you, too, will experience the joy I am feeling now."

"What's that, Charlie?" I asked.

He smiled and replied, "the total joy of witnessing God's love, his spirit marrying itself in a person's heart. Like a flower bursting into a bloom, its beauty radiates for all to see. In two short months I have witnessed the rebirth of your spirit, and watched your inner-self be transformed. I've seen a young man filled with doubt; blossom into a man filled with strength and confidence due to his new faith and love in God. You have come a long way. Never doubt that God knew the turmoil you were in. That is why he kept tugging at your soul until you did something crazier than you'd ever done before. You came out here not really knowing why, a journey into the unknown, a journey that some back home will question your very sanity. Ryan, everything in life happens for a purpose. Unfortunately, many people ignore the circumstances in their lives and too many times shrug off important crossroads in their lives as coincidences."

The old man looked at me with a seriousness I hadn't seen before. "Son, hear me when I say there are no coincidences in life. Everything, every person we meet, every circumstance that passes through our lives has a purpose. Many times it is God's way of communicating with us, guiding us. The secret to joy and peace is to pay attention to the events in our lives, no matter how small. God orchestrates the people and events that come into our lives for He is molding us into His purpose. He is trying to direct us to our destiny. And if we'll take time and talk to Him, ask Him what we are to learn from these meetings, these circumstances, He will give us the answers. God will provide us with clarity and understanding if we take time each day and pray to Him."

"Son," he said, looking into my eyes, "I have come into your life for a reason, and you into mine. Now we could be like many people and ignore our chance meeting, or we can accept the fact that we were brought together for His purpose. Do you understand what I'm saying, Ryan?" His words were profound. And I understood their meaning.

"Yes, Charlie," I answered. "I think I do. There were times when I first arrived I just wanted to leave, for I was frightened by the mystery in all of this and you. But a voice inside me kept telling me to stay and through our time together in prayer, and discussions, I knew I couldn't leave. I didn't understand, but deep down I knew God brought me here."

"Oh, bless you, bless you," he said, his voice raising. "That is the power of faith. Never forget this, Ryan. Faith in Him is everything, and God rewards our faith."

"The peace and joy you witness in me is founded in my undying faith in my Heavenly Father," the old man continued. "Oh, I don't know where he is taking me most of the time, but I always know that He loves me and watches over Me." He laughed and shook his head. "People complicate life so, and they look for answers in all the wrong places. All my wealth and material possessions never gave me a miniscule of the peace and joy that is a part of me now. That I owe to my relationship with God. Remember these truths, Ryan," he continued. "God never gives us more than we can handle and in Him is all we ever need. Carry these truths with you in life and worry will no longer exist."

I was in awe of this great man. His words stirred my heart and carried clarity of meaning deeper than I knew before.

"Charlie," I said, "then why is there so much suffering and evil in the world? Why do we choose to go down a darker road? I mean, what makes people do and act the way they do?"

He looked over his glasses, a sense of sadness in his face. "Because we are all born into this world sinners, all of us. It is our nature to be sinners, to be desirous of earthly things, things of the flesh. It's in our makeup. God knew that in giving us freedom of choice a new reality came with that. Life is the way it is because it is. Do you understand that, Ryan?" he asked.

"I'm not sure, Charlie," I answered, "you make it sound too simplistic." He thought for a moment.

"Look at it this way," he said. "How could you experience joy without knowing sadness? How could you experience health and healing without knowing sickness and disease? How could you experience love without knowing hate? Life is the way it is." This last statement he emphasized in a slow deliberate manner. "God knew in His infinite wisdom that for us to experience the beauty of life, to embrace and savor the feelings and emotions of love and kindness and compassion, all those glorious gifts of God, we had to be aware of their opposites."

I sat there mesmerized by the wisdom flowing forth from this wonderful old man, and to my surprise, it was making sense. Like a light going off, I sensed an understanding of God's brilliance in His creation.

Charlie stood and continued. "Son, understanding comes when we quit putting so much energy into questioning why, and start just feeling and believing. Faith brings to you understanding. One of the things Jesus witnessed during His short stay on earth was the weakness of our human nature. This is why he proclaimed "Fear not the world, for I have overcome the world." By the power of His faith and love for His Heavenly father He overcame the weakness of human nature. That precious and powerful gift God graces each and every one of us with. By trusting and loving Him, He will provide us all we will ever need to overcome the world. Yes, Ryan, by simple choice of worshipping our Heavenly father, by placing our trust and faith in Him, life on this planet, our relationship with one another would be gloriously transformed." The old man's voice was filled with excitement.

"Love, Ryan, is the most powerful force on earth. Do you know why?" he asked. He continued before I had a chance to answer. "Because love is the very essence of God. When we feel love we are experiencing Him. This is how great His love really is. Love is our direct connection to God. In each of us he gave our hearts the ability to love without end. Do you hear that, son?" he said, gesturing with his hands. "Our hearts have the capacity to love without limit. Oh, what a glorious gift He gave us. Ryan, can you even imagine the sheer glory of realizing our hearts have no bound in their ability to love? Oh," he said, raising his hands in the air, "Thank you, Lord, thank you."

I sat there dazed. Never had I heard Charlie speak with such conviction. He sat back down and smiled at me. "Love," he said "is a beautiful and precious gift from God. We all should give of it more freely."

He took a few deep breaths and continued. "Ryan, when problems and turmoil come into our lives, don't shrink from them in fear, but have faith in the knowledge that our problems are gifts from God in disguise." I looked at him.

"Huh," I said, under my voice.

"Think back and reflect on your life and those around you. Are we not strengthened by adversity? Do we not show compassion and love in crises? Many times our greatest spiritual growth comes during times of crises and turmoil. That is when God reveals that in Him is all we ever need." I thought of my grandmother who was blind for most of her adult life. She lived her life filled with more joy and peace than any of us with sight. She was a sight to behold. I don't think I ever remember her complaining about anything. She celebrated life with the love of God and Christ. She was always giving praise to Him. I smiled thinking back at how happy she was in her life. I didn't appreciate the power of her faith in God as a child, but the impact was hitting me now. How I wished I would have taken the time as an adult to spend more time with her and allowed her to share her joy in Christ with me. A sense of sadness came over me for I had always been too busy with my life to spend more time with her. In many ways she reminded me of Charlie, for she, too, had that inner peace and joy. The loss and missed opportunity brought tears to my eyes.

Charlie noticed my emotions. "What is it son?" he asked.

"Oh, nothing, I was just thinking of my grandmother and the joy and peace that were a part of her because of her love and faith in God. The old man smiled. "Ryan, we witness the glory of His love in people's lives every day. Everyday we hear of miracles, witness the wondrous transformation of the human spirit, and still people doubt and don't believe. They have little faith, how sad," he said, shaking his head.

"Charlie," I said, still filled with emotion, "will I have the strength and courage that she had if I lost my sight?" A strange calmness settled over me as I spoke those words. When I received news of my eye disease, of having RP and that it would slowly rob me of my sight, it shook me to the core. But now a quiet calm was over me. How different I felt.

He gently put his hands on mine. Looking into my eyes, he spoke softly. "Son, I know how devastating it was for you getting your news of your eye disease. I know you don't understand this now, but you will. Through your new faith and love in Him, his plan will become clear when the time is right. He squeezed my hands. "Son, hold onto that truth and never let go of it. Remember how much He loves you, that in Him is all you'll ever need. He has chosen to use you for some very special reason."

I so believed and trusted this old man that his words comforted me and brought me peace. I nodded my head that I understood.

Charlie got up and went inside, saying he'd be back out in a moment. Darkness had set upon us a good while ago. I put more wood on the fire until it burned brightly. Charlie appeared holding two glasses of his special tea. He walked over next to me and handed me a glass. I smiled at him, for this was always a special treat for Charlie. He truly enjoyed sharing his special drink.

He raised his glass to mine. "To you, Ryan, my dear and trusted friend. May we drink to your safe voyage home? It is time," he said, "for you to go home." Our glasses clinked together as we slowly sipped the heavenly nectar. I stared at Charlie, not sure what to say. This place, his home, had become a special sanctuary to me. It felt strange to think of leaving. Finally I forced out the words, "Are you sure? Am I really ready to go home?"

He smiled with a look of love and kindness in his eyes. 'Yes, Ryan, my son. You are ready to go home. You have people who love you waiting back home," he said. "It's time for you to allow them the joy of knowing the new you. Share with them in celebrating your rebirth, your new appreciation for the precious gift of life. Welcome them into your arms and feel the love and strength of your relationship with God. Oh, the wonderful life that awaits you, son. Hallelujah, thank you God," he shouted into the night air. He was filled with excitement and joy and I was too. He put his arm around my shoulders. "And ask that sweet lady to marry you before she slips away, before she realizes the bum you really are," he said, laughing, giving me a wink. We laughed.

We sat gazing up at the starry night sky. It was a night sky like I had never seen before. There were hundreds, thousands of stars sparkling in the night sky. Never in all my years had my poor night vision allowed me to witness such a glorious sky. Maybe it was the clear Montana sky that brought this spectacular sight into view, or maybe it was God's gift to me to allow me to see beyond my sight.

"Hallelujah, hallelujah," I shouted. "Thank you Lord, thank you." Charlie looked at me. "Oh, Charlie, isn't it just beautiful, isn't it wonderful?" I couldn't hide my excitement. "Never have I seen a star filled sky like this. Life is truly a miracle and a wonder to behold." I raised my glass. "To new life, Charlie."

"To new life," he repeated. We spent several hours talking and gazing into the heavens. Several falling stars streaked across the black sky that was above us. My thoughts turned to home. Suddenly I was overwhelmed at how much I had missed everyone. I couldn't wait to have Sarah in my arms, or to see the smiles and hear the screams of excitement from my son. I truly was a man blessed.

It had been a long day and Charlie had shared so much with me. I was exhausted. Charlie carried our glasses inside while I put out the fire. I thanked Charlie for a very special day, gave him a big hug and bid him goodnight. I crawled in bed, Red jumping up with me. "Boy, we're going home," I said patting his head. I quickly fell off to sleep.

CHAPTER 13

The next day was filled with a mixture of emotions. I was happy at the thought of seeing everyone back home, but yet sad at leaving this special place and leaving Charlie. I savored every precious moment of this day, for I would be heading home tomorrow. On this morning as we spent time at the altar, we both gave prayers of thanks for all our blessings. Charlie prayed for my safe passage home. We returned to the cabin and did our daily reading. Charlie was unusually upbeat this day.

We drove into town so I could call home with the news I was on my way home. My son screamed with excitement at the news and Sara burst into tears. I told them I should be home late Friday afternoon. Sarah informed me she was taking the day off in preparation for my homecoming. I told her not to plan anything elaborate because I wanted a private time with her and my son. She replied that was fine. I really was a blessed man. I didn't call work, for I figured I would cross that bridge once I was back. I doubted a couple of days would matter one way or another.

I purchased some snacks and drinks for my journey and thanked Big Jim for his hospitality and kindness. He gave me a firm handshake and said it was a pleasure meeting me.

On the drive back to Charlie's place, I was lost in a sea of thoughts. I had grown to love this place and this dear old man. I knew I would sorely miss him. I wondered how all the changes in me would carry home. Charlie's Woods had been a sacred sanctuary for me. What would happen with me when I left here, I didn't know.

"You are unusually quiet today," Charlie finally said. "Is everything okay, Ryan?"

"I'm okay Charlie," I said, somewhat sadly. "Just a mixed bag of emotions today."

"I understand," he replied, smiling at me.

"Charlie, I'm going to miss you so much," I said.

"And I'll miss you, too," he said, "but know that even though we'll be physically apart, spiritually we will be bound together for the rest of our lives. So you see, we really won't be apart." His words comforted me and finally I smiled back. "That's better," he said with a bellowing voice. "It is a glorious day."

I laughed. "Yes it is, Charlie. Yes it is."

After lunch we walked to the gorge to spend one last afternoon together there. We reveled in being alive and just enjoyed the beauty of our surroundings. We watched Red chase birds and butterflies and laughed at his playfulness.

That evening I cooked Charlie dinner. He sat back and teased me as I prepared our meal. As we ate, we enjoyed pleasant conversation. "Everything is very good," the old man commented, "but I knew it would be."

"I'm glad you enjoyed it," I replied.

"Charlie, how do I ever repay you for all that you have done for me?" He sat there for a moment, rubbing his chin as if deep in thought. He was quiet for the longest time, and when he spoke I was shocked by his words.

"Ryan, writing comes pretty natural for you, doesn't it?"

"I'm not sure what you're asking me," I replied.

"Well, I mean it's easy for you to express yourself, your feelings in words, isn't it?"

"Well, yes," I said. "It was one of my strong points in school and college, but why are you asking me all this?"

"Well, you remember me saying that you were blessed with a gift, and you told me that you had no idea what it was?"

"Yes," I said, wondering what he was getting at.

"That's it, that's it Ryan!" his voice filled with excitement.

"What, Charlie, what's it?" I said, perplexed by his sudden excitement.

"Write," he said.

"What do you mean, right?" I said, shaking my head.

"Ryan, write," he said, motioning with his hand, his thumb and forefinger pressed together.

"Oh, write," I said, but I was still confused.

His excitement grew. "Oh, hallelujah, thank you, Lord, you have patience with him Lord, he's just a rookie."

"Charlie," I yelled, "what in the world are you talking about? Fill me in," I said, gesturing with my hand. His exuberance made me laugh.

"I told you, you would have your answers before you left here," he said. "You are to write for people to read."

"Write what, Charlie?" I asked. "What could I possibly write that people would want to read?" I said empathetically.

"Oh, ye of little faith," he said. "Rookie," he joked, "well, first off you'll have plenty of time since you said you most likely don't have a job."

"Oh, shoot, thanks, Charlie," I said, "you're making me feel better."

"Faith, Ryan, remember you are on a journey of faith," he said, pointing a finger at me.

He stared into my eyes; seriousness came over his face and in his voice. "Write about your experience here, your thoughts and feelings. All of it Ryan, put it in paper, put it in a book. He then made a revelation that I wouldn't understand or fully appreciate until later.

"Son," he said the seriousness in his voice still there, "this is His purpose for you, the path He wishes you to travel. Remember the voice in your dream, Ryan," excitement returning to his voice. "Trust in Me, and stay to the path I've put you on. Oh, hallelujah!" he shouted, lifting his eyes to the heavens.

"Son, God is guiding your life and your destiny, now have faith and listen, listen."

The old man was so emphatic about this, and to my surprise, believed all of it. At this moment I didn't know how, I didn't have a clue, but in my gut I believed what Charlie was telling me. "Son, many, many will benefit from sharing your experience. Oh, the good that it will do, the seeds of hope it will sow. Glory be to God," he said, closing his eyes. "Glory be to God," he repeated, softly. If Charlie believed sharing my experience would truly help people, then I was willing to write about it.

"Son, know that He loves you and watches over you, and guides you. God doesn't give bad advice," he said, with a smile. "Remember, there will be many times along your journey that the negative forces of life will try to distract you from your chosen path and cloud your vision. Do not allow them to throw you off course, walk steadfastly along your path armed with the power of your faith and the vision of His glory will always be in front of you to see. If God be for you, then fear nothing that be against you. Remember these words by the apostle Paul to the Romans, for carry the strength of truth.

"For I am persuaded, that neither death, nor life, nor angels, nor principalities, nor powers, nor things present, nor things to come, nor height, nor depth, not any other creature shall be able to separate us from the love of God, which is in Jesus Christ our Lord."

"Ryan," he said, placing his hands on mine, "carry these truths forever in your heart. Feel, experience His boundless love for you and all people, strengthen your faith by praying to Him everyday, take time to be still and listen to His voice. Do these things and your life will be blessed beyond your wildest dreams."

He smiled and paused. "Our work here is finished for now, and you have the answers you sought. Let us pray and give thanks," he said.

Charlie's Woods

As we said Amen, I felt totally overwhelmed form this evening's events. I sat back in my chair, closed my eyes, taking deep slow breaths, trying to calm myself down.

Charlie poured us our last special tea to share together. We spent the rest of the evening reminiscing about our time together. We laughed and we cried.

Finally, he said it was time to retire for the evening. He gave me a long hug. "You have a long journey ahead of you, so get a good night sleep." He said he loved me, then said goodnight. I sat staring into the fire. I was still in awe of what transpired this evening. I was truly heading in a new direction. I still could barely believe everything that had occurred over these past two months. I truly was a blessed man. And what to make of Charlie, he was unlike anybody I had ever met in my life. I was convinced he had a mystical supernatural quality and yes, as hard as it might be to believe, a direct connection to God. I was tired and pulled the blanket off the rocker. I lay down by the fireplace next to Red, who was already asleep. I pulled the blanket over both of us and drifted off into peaceful slumber.

CHAPTER 14

Apparently more tired than I realized, I didn't even awaken until ten the next morning. The fire was now a pile of smoldering embers. My aches and pains quickly reminded me that sleeping on the floor had lost the comfort it held in my youth. Red greeted me with his usual exuberance, licking my cheek and barking. I opened the door to let him out. I suddenly noticed a strange silence to the cabin. Charlie should have been up by now. I could smell the aroma of coffee brewing. I washed my face and brushed my teeth. I walked outside to see if I could find Charlie. His truck was gone. Odd, I thought, he didn't say anything to me about going anywhere this morning.

I let Red back in and walked into the kitchen to pour myself a cup of coffee. There on the counter were some Danish and a note. I carried my coffee, Danish and the note to the table and sat down, after taking as few sips of coffee and bites of Danish, I unfolded the note:

"Dear Ryan, I apologize for not being able to see you off." My mouth dropped open and a sinking feeling came over my heart.

"Something important came up which needed my attention. It's hard to find the words to express my joy for the time we spent together. I will never forget the special person you are or the special friendship we shared. Please do not be disheartened by my absence this day. I will cherish forever in my heart the time we spent together. May you share with the world your new

101

life, love and knowledge of our brotherhood. You will be a ray of light in a dark world. Stay true to your destiny, have faith and trust in God and your light will be added to millions of others to brighten our world. I will see you again but not for awhile. You are welcome back here anytime. Leave no obstacle stand in your way of writing your book for many would be cheated of benefiting from your experience. Take time every day to be still and visit with God and He will guide you all the way. Please accept the gift I left you in your car as an expression of my love for you. God bless you. Charlie."

Disappointed about his absence, I quietly packed my things, struggling to fight back the tears. As I sat everything on the porch, Red and I made one last walk to the old man's altar. It wasn't the same without him. I knelt down on my knees and gave thanks to God. As we headed back to the cabin, I savored every step, every breath. What a different man I had become. Gone were all my fears and insecurities. As I packed the car I knew I would sorely miss the old man and his woods. Though my life had been turned inside out, I now walked with a deep sense of peace and purpose. I yelled thanks and goodbye to Charlie, for part of him was in these woods. I opened the driver's door and Red jumped in. I stared in disbelief, remembering the present he said he left in his note. There on the seat was his precious Bible. As I held this special, special book to my chest, I began to cry. "Charlie, Charlie, why, why me?" All my emotions and gratitude flowed forth. As I pressed his precious gift to my lips, I felt his presence all around me. I turned around, but no one was there. My tears turned to laughter as I thought of that grin that I was sure was on Charlie's face.

I wrapped the Bible on one of my old shirts and tucked it carefully in my suitcase. I climbed in, shut my door, and turned the key. As I started to pull away, I paused and looked back at the cabin that had become a refuge. "Thank you, Charlie," I said quietly. "Thank you for showing me a new life." As we slowly drove away, I was anxious to go home, but couldn't help but wonder what the future had in store for me.

EPILOGUE

So much has happened to me since I arrived home from Charlie's Woods. I married Sara, bought a business, and yes, wrote this book. Considering the broken man I was two years ago, these accomplishments in my life are monumental

None of this would have been possible without my new life in Jesus Christ and the wondrous teachings of my dear friend Charlie. These are the pillars of strength on which I have built my new life upon.

The writing of this book was a major challenge for me. There were many days when completing it became a real struggle. When doubts about my writing ability would creep in and the words would cease to flow. But then I would feel the old man's presence and hear his bellowing voice reminding me that many would benefit from the sharing of my story.

I prayed to God often during these times to help me find the right words, to give me strength to persevere.

So I share my story of hope to all who yearn for a more meaningful life, to those whose lives are filled with pain, suffering, heartache, hopelessness and despair. If you truly desire to free yourself from the yoke that imprisons your life, then now is the time to surrender yourself to Jesus Christ.

Allow His love, His spirit to envelope you and He will lift the yoke from your shoulders that now paralyzes you. Embrace the power of Christ's love and your life will be miraculously transformed as mine was.

My story is a testimony to the awesome power and depth of God's love. Know that God's love is given by grace and not by works. His love is given freely to anyone who truly seeks it. God's love is real, unconditional and eternal.

Imagine your new life armored with the love of God. What force on Earth can stand against you?

The Apostle Paul declared in Romans Chapter 8:38 and 39, "For I am persuaded that neither death nor life, nor angels, nor principalities, nor power, nor things present, nor things to come. Nor height, nor depth, nor any other creature shall be able to separate us from the love of God which is in Christ Jesus our Lord."

Walk confidently in God's light knowing that our greatest power lies in the power of prayer and that nothing in this world can separate you from the love of God.

As I lay my pen down I pray my dear old friend is proud of the book I have written.